Common Core Writing Handbook

Teacher's Guide

GRADE

5

Photo Credits

Placement Key: (r) right, (l) left, (c) center, (t) top, (b) bottom, (bg) background

Front cover (cl) PhotoAlto/Getty Images; (tr) Photodisc/Getty Images; (bl) Photodisc/Getty Images; (cr) Comstock/Getty Images; (bc) Image Source/Getty Images.

Back cover (tl) Photodisc/Getty Images; (cl) Photodisc/Getty Images; (cr) Comstock/Getty Images; (br) Adobe Image Library/Getty Images.

Printed in the U.S.A.

ISBN: 978-0-547-86517-1

15 16 0928 21 20 19 18 17 16

4500595362   B C D E F G

HOUGHTON MIFFLIN HARCOURT

Contents

Writing Strategies

How to Use This Book

The *Common Core Writing Handbook* was designed to complement the writing instruction in your reading program as well as meet all of the Common Core State Standards for writing. It consists of two components: a handbook for students that they can refer to as a resource as well as practice writing in throughout the year, and a Teacher's Guide that supports instruction by providing minilessons for every handbook topic.

Components

Two easy-to-use components make up the *Common Core Writing Handbook* program:

- For Grades 2–6, a 160-page partially consumable student handbook with 30 writing topics that correlate to your reading program's key writing lessons.

  The first section of each grade-level handbook includes writing models along with interactive practice to scaffold or reinforce students' understanding of opinion, informational/explanatory, and narrative writing. As students practice writing, they build additional examples of forms to refer to throughout the year as well as develop a deeper understanding of each form's structure.

  The second section of the handbook is a resource tool that students can refer to whenever they write. Topics range from writing strategies to how to use technology to do research.

- For Grade 1, a 96-page partially consumable student handbook also includes 30 correlated handbook topics followed by a resource section on writing strategies, such as the writing process and writing traits.

- For Grades K–6, a Teacher's Guide with 60 minilessons for section 1 (two minilessons for each section 1 student handbook topic) plus one minilesson, as needed, for each remaining page of the resource handbook. The Kindergarten Teacher's Guide includes an abundance of copying masters.

Minilessons

Minilessons are short, focused lessons on specific topics. For each minilesson, you will demonstrate an aspect of writing before students try their own hand. In this Teacher's Guide, minilessons are provided for each topic in the handbook. In the first section are two minilessons for each topic. Each of these minilessons consists of the following parts:

- Topic title
- Tab with section name
- Minilesson number and title.
- Common Core State Standards
- Objective and guiding question
- Easy-to-follow instruction in an *I Do*, *We Do*, and *You Do* format
- Modeled, collaborative, and independent writing
- Conference and evaluation information

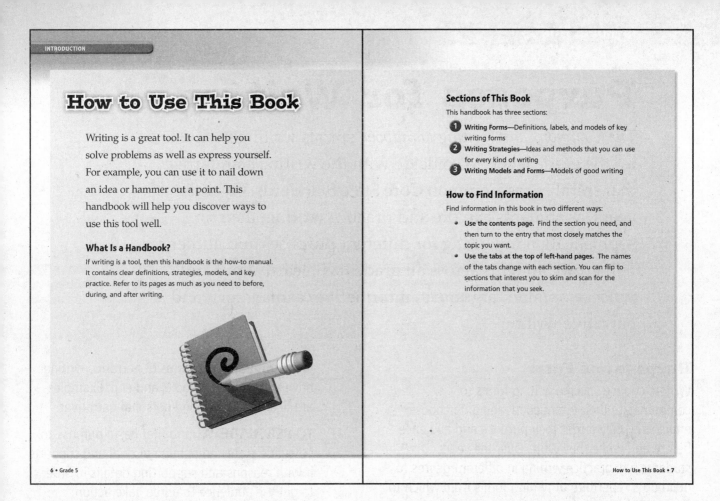

How to Use This Book

Writing is a great tool! It can help you solve problems as well as express yourself. For example, you can use it to nail down an idea or hammer out a point. This handbook will help you discover ways to use this tool well.

What Is a Handbook?

If writing is a tool, then this handbook is the how-to manual. It contains clear definitions, strategies, models, and key practice. Refer to its pages as much as you need to before, during, and after writing.

Sections of This Book

This handbook has three sections:

1. **Writing Forms**—Definitions, labels, and models of key writing forms
2. **Writing Strategies**—Ideas and methods that you can use for every kind of writing
3. **Writing Models and Forms**—Models of good writing

How to Find Information

Find information in this book in two different ways:

- **Use the contents page.** Find the section you need, and then turn to the entry that most closely matches the topic you want.
- **Use the tabs at the top of left-hand pages.** The names of the tabs change with each section. You can flip to sections that interest you to skim and scan for the information that you seek.

- Technology references
- Reduced facsimiles of student handbook pages
- Tips for corrective feedback
- A feature that further explores the lesson's writing trait

Each writing minilesson has been correlated to your reading program's writing lessons so that all minilessons and corresponding writing handbook pages within this section are used at least once during the school year. Additional minilessons are provided throughout the Teacher's Guide and correlate to each remaining page in the handbook. Use these minilessons, as needed, to clarify concepts for students and provide additional support.

Student-Page Walk-Through

Have students turn to and read pages 6 and 7 in their books. Explain to them that their handbook is a tool that they can use whenever they write. It can help them find information quickly about any writing question they have, and they can use it to help them during writing. Guide students to find each of these parts in their handbooks:

- Table of contents
- Introductory pages, including overviews of the writing process and the writing traits
- Writing form pages, each with a section tab, title, definition, and helpful bulleted points, followed by a clear example of the writing model as well as a write-in activity page
- Additional reference pages on topics ranging from writing strategies to revising to using technology, as well as more examples of writing models they may need or want to refer to during the year for projects and other assignments
- An index. Remind students that the table of contents is in order of presentation while the index is ordered alphabetically.

Purposes for Writing

The Common Core Writing Handbook spirals writing instruction up the grade levels to coincide with the writing standards that spiral in the Common Core State Standards. Over the years, as students explore and practice writing, their sophistication in writing for different purposes and audiences will grow. Students across all grades will learn about and practice opinion/argument, informative/explanatory, and narrative writing.

Purpose and Form

Writers choose specific writing forms to communicate their intended meaning. To choose effectively, they target their purpose and audience before and while they write. Over the years, students will practice writing in different genres to build up a repertoire of writing forms from which to choose. This increasing practice as well as access to information about writing will help students feel more comfortable about writing and, hopefully, enjoy doing it.

In this handbook, the writing forms and models presented coincide primarily with the purposes expressed through the Common Core State Standards. These are to inform, to explain, to narrate, and to persuade. There are other purposes for writing as well, but these four are emphasized to best prepare students for college and career readiness.

TO INFORM The purpose for writing to inform is to share facts and other information. Informational texts such as reports make statements that are supported by facts and truthful evidence.

TO EXPLAIN The purpose for writing to explain is to tell *what, how,* and *why* about a topic. An example is to explain in writing how to do or make something.

TO NARRATE The purpose of writing to narrate is to tell a story. The story can be made up or truthful. Most forms of narrative writing have a beginning, middle, and end. Examples are fictional stories and personal narratives.

TO PERSUADE Writing that has a purpose to persuade states an opinion or goal and supports it with reasons and supporting details in order to get the audience to agree, take action, or both. At Grade 6, the emphasis shifts to argument.

Over the years, as their writing grows more sophisticated, students may find that their purpose for writing is a hybrid of two or more purposes. An example would be literary nonfiction that includes elements of storytelling although it may be written primarily to inform and explain. Another example would be historical fiction that tells a story but relates events accurately in order to inform the reader as well.

Success in School and Life

Students and adults are often judged by how well they can communicate. Students are encouraged to learn to write effectively to be successful in their studies. In particular, by the upper grades, they need to master the basic essay format that includes:

- An introductory paragraph that identifies the topic or statement of purpose.

- Supporting paragraphs that provide related details and examples.

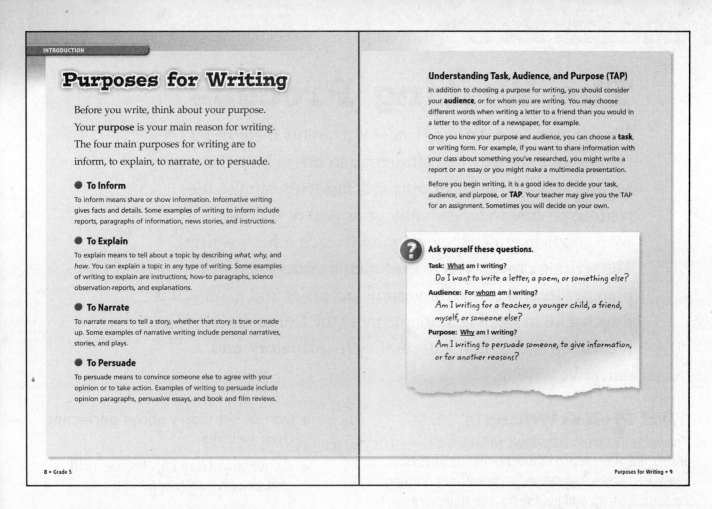

Purposes for Writing

Before you write, think about your purpose. Your **purpose** is your main reason for writing. The four main purposes for writing are to inform, to explain, to narrate, or to persuade.

● To Inform

To inform means share or show information. Informative writing gives facts and details. Some examples of writing to inform include reports, paragraphs of information, news stories, and instructions.

● To Explain

To explain means to tell about a topic by describing *what, why,* and *how.* You can explain a topic in any type of writing. Some examples of writing to explain are instructions, how-to paragraphs, science observation reports, and explanations.

● To Narrate

To narrate means to tell a story, whether that story is true or made up. Some examples of narrative writing include personal narratives, stories, and plays.

● To Persuade

To persuade means to convince someone else to agree with your opinion or to take action. Examples of writing to persuade include opinion paragraphs, persuasive essays, and book and film reviews.

Understanding Task, Audience, and Purpose (TAP)

In addition to choosing a purpose for writing, you should consider your **audience**, or for whom you are writing. You may choose different words when writing a letter to a friend than you would in a letter to the editor of a newspaper, for example.

Once you know your purpose and audience, you can choose a **task**, or writing form. For example, if you want to share information with your class about something you've researched, you might write a report or an essay or you might make a multimedia presentation.

Before you begin writing, it is a good idea to decide your task, audience, and purpose, or **TAP**. Your teacher may give you the TAP for an assignment. Sometimes you will decide on your own.

> **?** **Ask yourself these questions.**
>
> **Task:** <u>What</u> am I writing?
> *Do I want to write a letter, a poem, or something else?*
>
> **Audience:** For <u>whom</u> am I writing?
> *Am I writing for a teacher, a younger child, a friend, myself, or someone else?*
>
> **Purpose:** <u>Why</u> am I writing?
> *Am I writing to persuade someone, to give information, or for another reasons?*

- A closing paragraph that sums up and concludes.

Students will use this essay form to produce reports, literary analyses, theses, and critiques throughout their academic career. They will also be tested on their ability to write effective essays in standardized tests. In later life, as adults, they will need to be able to communicate clearly in writing to coworkers, bosses, and clients. This requires extensive and ongoing exposure to exemplary writing models and explicit instruction in a variety of areas, as well as opportunities to practice different forms of writing. In all cases, their purpose for writing must be clear. Evidence suggests that the more time student writers spend on writing, developing their writing skills, and deepening their writing experience, the better writers they become.

The Reading-Writing Connection

The ability to communicate their thinking about texts for a variety of purposes and audiences will serve students well in preparation for college and career readiness. When students write about what they read, reflecting on content, craft, or another aspect of a text, they provide evidence of their thinking. This helps teachers know how well students have understood a text. Additionally, the more students write in response to texts, the more they increase their ability to reflect and improve their critical writing ability. Also, students learn to cite evidence from texts in supporting their claims or supporting their main ideas. This ability becomes particularly useful in writing reports and opinion pieces.

Introduce the Purposes

Have students turn to page 8 and read the text. Explain that these are the key purposes for writing that will be explored in their handbooks. Give or elicit an example of a writing form that might be used for each purpose. Examples might include an informational paragraph or a research report *to inform,* directions or a how-to essay *to explain,* a story or personal narrative *to narrate,* and an opinion essay or letter to the editor *to persuade.* Then have students read the next page. Discuss how students should always consider their TAP—or task, audience, and purpose—to help them better target the message of their writing.

The Writing Process

The Common Core Writing Handbook presents the writing process as a strategy that students can use to help them write for any task, audience, or purpose. Students can use the writing process independently or as part of writing workshops in which they respond to each other's writing. The writing process can help students understand how to plan, write, and revise for various purposes and genres. It is thus useful in helping students meet the Common Core State Standards for opinion, informative/explanatory, and narrative writing.

What Process Writing Is

The writing process, or process writing, is an instructional approach to writing that consists of five basic stages. The stages are prewriting, drafting, revising, editing, and publishing. The stages are recursive in nature, meaning that students are encouraged to go back and forth between the stages as needed.

The characteristics of the stages of the writing process are as follows:

Prewriting

This is the stage where students begin to plan their writing. Students:

- Define a task and purpose.
- Identify an audience.
- Brainstorm ideas.
- Narrow and choose a topic.
- Plan and organize information.

Drafting

During drafting, students make their first attempt at fleshing out the prewriting idea and forming it into a written work. In other words, students put their ideas in writing. In this stage, students:

- Write a first draft.

- Do not yet worry about perfecting their writing.
- Know that they can revise, edit, and proofread later.
- Use their plan and checklists to help them write or to return to prewriting, as needed.

Revising

A draft is reread and decisions are made to rework and improve it. In this stage, students might:

- Read aloud their work to others to determine how it sounds and how it might be improved.
- Conference with other students.
- Add information.
- Delete unnecessary information.
- Rearrange sentences.
- Combine sentences.

Editing

During editing, the draft is polished. In this stage, students reread and correct their writing for:

- Grammar
- Spelling

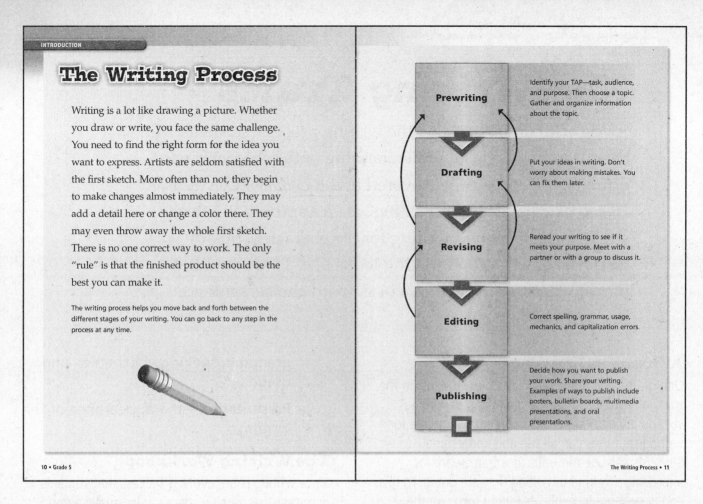

The Writing Process

Writing is a lot like drawing a picture. Whether you draw or write, you face the same challenge. You need to find the right form for the idea you want to express. Artists are seldom satisfied with the first sketch. More often than not, they begin to make changes almost immediately. They may add a detail here or change a color there. They may even throw away the whole first sketch. There is no one correct way to work. The only "rule" is that the finished product should be the best you can make it.

The writing process helps you move back and forth between the different stages of your writing. You can go back to any step in the process at any time.

Prewriting
Identify your TAP—task, audience, and purpose. Then choose a topic. Gather and organize information about the topic.

Drafting
Put your ideas in writing. Don't worry about making mistakes. You can fix them later.

Revising
Reread your writing to see if it meets your purpose. Meet with a partner or with a group to discuss it.

Editing
Correct spelling, grammar, usage, mechanics, and capitalization errors.

Publishing
Decide how you want to publish your work. Share your writing. Examples of ways to publish include posters, bulletin boards, multimedia presentations, and oral presentations.

- Mechanics
- Usage

Publishing

Students share their writing with others. In this stage, students typically:

- Make a final, clean copy.
- Use their best handwriting, if writing by hand. If they are sharing their work electronically, they typically choose typefaces and other elements to make their writing readable and attractive.
- Combine their writing with art or graphics.
- Make multiple copies, read their writing aloud, post it electronically, or share or display it in another way.

Introduce the Process

Have students read pages 10–11. Explain that the writing process is a strategy that they can use to help them write about any topic. Point out how the graphic on page 11 has arrows, indicating that students can go back and forth between the stages as needed. For students who have no previous orientation to the writing process, simplify your introduction by emphasizing at first only the three key stages of planning, drafting, and revising. Elicit how most tasks of any nature require planning, doing or making something, and then thinking about what might be done better and making those improvements. Compare how these same basic stages can be used each time students write.

Have students turn to the table of contents and locate the section in their handbooks devoted to the writing process (p. 74-81). Explain that they can use these handbook pages whenever they need help with specific stages or writing in general. Point out that each stage in the handbook has one or two pages devoted to it that tell more about the stage. As an example, have students turn to the Prewriting pages 74-75, and point out how they show the different organizational plans students can use for the different kinds of writing they will do. Encourage students to use their handbooks as a resource whenever they write.

The Writing Traits

Along with understanding the writing process, students will benefit from having an understanding of the characteristics, or traits, of good writing covered in the *Common Core Writing Handbook*. The "Traits of Writing" is an approach in which students analyze their writing for the characteristics, or qualities, of what good writing looks like. These qualities include ideas, organization, voice, word choice, sentence fluency, and conventions.

A Common Language

One of the advantages of instructing students in the traits of writing is that you give them a working vocabulary and thus build a common language for writing that they can all use and understand. Students can use the traits as a framework for improving any kind of writing they are doing. To this end, a systematic, explicitly taught focus on the traits of writing has proved to be an effective tool for discussing writing, enabling students to analyze and improve their own writing, and providing teachers with a way to assess students' compositions in a fair, even-handed manner.

Writers typically focus on six traits, with presentation—or the appearance of writing— sometimes considered an additional trait.

- **Ideas**—the meaning and development of the message.
- **Organization**—the structure of the writing.
- **Voice**—the tone of the writing, which reveals the writer's personality and affects the audience's interpretation of the message.
- **Word Choice**—the words the writer uses to convey the message.
- **Sentence Fluency**—the flow and rhythm of the writing.
- **Conventions**—the correctness of the grammar, spelling, mechanics, and usage.
- **Presentation**—the appearance of the writing.

The Writing Workshop

Since writing is an involved process that students accomplish at varying speeds, it is usually a good idea to set aside a block of time for them to work on their writing. One time-tested model that has worked well in classrooms is the Writing Workshop. In this model during a set period of time, students work individually and collaboratively (with classmates and/or with the teacher) on different writing activities. One of these activities is for students to collaborate in reviewing each other's manuscripts. One effective technique used in many workshops as a way for students to comment on aspects of each other's writing is to use the language of the traits when they comment.

Some tasks are started and finished during a workshop, whiles others are ongoing. A writing workshop can serve many writing-related functions:

- Students can work on a class writing assignment (ongoing or quickly accomplished).
- Students can engage in independent writing, jotting down or consulting ideas in their writing log or journal, starting or working on pieces of their own devising.

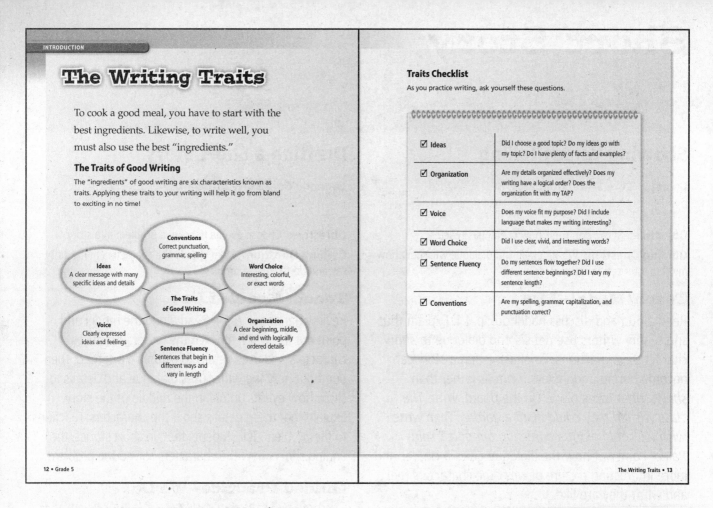

The Writing Traits

To cook a good meal, you have to start with the best ingredients. Likewise, to write well, you must also use the best "ingredients."

The Traits of Good Writing

The "ingredients" of good writing are six characteristics known as traits. Applying these traits to your writing will help it go from bland to exciting in no time!

Conventions
Correct punctuation, grammar, spelling

Ideas
A clear message with many specific ideas and details

Word Choice
Interesting, colorful, or exact words

The Traits of Good Writing

Voice
Clearly expressed ideas and feelings

Organization
A clear beginning, middle, and end with logically ordered details

Sentence Fluency
Sentences that begin in different ways and vary in length

Traits Checklist

As you practice writing, ask yourself these questions.

☑ Ideas	Did I choose a good topic? Do my ideas go with my topic? Do I have plenty of facts and examples?
☑ Organization	Are my details organized effectively? Does my writing have a logical order? Does the organization fit with my TAP?
☑ Voice	Does my voice fit my purpose? Did I include language that makes my writing interesting?
☑ Word Choice	Did I use clear, vivid, and interesting words?
☑ Sentence Fluency	Do my sentences flow together? Did I use different sentence beginnings? Did I vary my sentence length?
☑ Conventions	Are my spelling, grammar, capitalization, and punctuation correct?

- As previously mentioned, students can engage in peer-conferencing, giving one another advice about a piece of writing or sharing writing ideas.

- Students can select pieces for inclusion in their writing portfolio, where they keep their best work.

- Teachers can conference with individual students, reviewing student writing and discussing a given student's strengths and weaknesses as well as instructional progress.

- Teachers can engage in small-group instruction with students who need extra help with practice in specific areas of writing.

Writing Workshops are often most effective when they adhere to a dependable schedule and follow a set of clearly posted guidelines (for example, keep voices down, point out the good things about someone's writing as well as comment on aspects that might be revised, listen politely, put away materials when the workshop is over). In addition, students should know what areas of the classroom they can use during the Workshop and should have free access to writing materials, including their handbooks.

You may want to refer to the Writing Workshop pages in this *Common Core Writing Handbook Teacher's Guide* and teach one or two minilessons on writing workshop behaviors and activities so that students have a solid understanding of what is expected of them.

Introduce the Traits

Share the Writing Traits overview pages with students. Discuss each trait briefly and explain to students that their handbooks contain more information on the traits, which they can use as they plan, draft, revise, edit, and publish their writing. Guide students to use their tables of contents or indexes to locate where additional information can be found in their handbooks.

Short Story

Minilesson 1	Minilesson 2

Showing Versus Telling

Common Core State Standards: W.5.3b, W.5.3d

Objective: Show, don't tell, how characters react.

Guiding Question: What details and dialogue will show how my character reacts in my story?

Teach/Model—I Do

Read aloud and discuss handbook p. 14. Explain that short story writers use details and dialogue to *show* characters and actions. Emphasize that a story can become boring and lifeless if it *tells* rather than *shows* what takes place. On the board, write *The class wished they could plant a garden.* Then write *"I wish we could plant a garden in our pod,"* said *Paulo.* Point out how the dialogue gives a clearer and more interesting picture of what the characters feel and what they are like.

Guided Practice—We Do

On the board, write a title for a short story that sets up a problem, such as *The Girl Who Couldn't Skateboard.* Work with students to write five things the main character can say that show how she feels about the problem set up in the title, such as *"Why can't I keep my balance on this thing?"*

Practice/Apply—You Do

COLLABORATIVE Write other titles for short stories, such as *The Town That Survived the Storm* or *The Dog That Would Not Obey.* Have groups choose one idea and write five sentences the main character might say about the problem. Remind students to use dialogue to show how the character feels.

INDEPENDENT Have students choose another short story title from the list and write five lines of dialogue that show how the character feels about the problem.

Conference/Evaluate

Have students evaluate their dialogue to make sure it shows how characters react to the problem.

Drafting a Short Story

Common Core State Standards: W.5.3a, W.5.3e

Objective: Choose events to solve a problem in a story.

Guiding Question: What should the characters in my story say and do to solve a problem?

Teach/Model—I Do

Review handbook p. 14. Read aloud the model and point out the ways in which the writer introduces characters and uses details to establish a setting. Then point out how the writer uses dialogue and details to show how events unfold in the middle of the story. Explain that these details show the characters' reactions to the problem. Tell students that, in short stories, the ending shows how the characters solved the problem.

Guided Practice—We Do

 Direct students to the frame on handbook p. 15. Tell them that you will work together to write a short story about a bear cub. Help students create dialogue and events that show the main character's reaction to the problem. For example, *The frustrated little bear cub shouted, "Help! My paw is stuck!"* Brainstorm solutions with students. Have them write a draft in their books as you write on the board.

Practice/Apply—You Do

 COLLABORATIVE Have groups plan and complete Activity 2. Tell them to think of what the character would say or do in the situation. Have groups share what they have written.

 INDEPENDENT Have students read and follow the directions. Tell them to use their prewriting plan from Lesson 1 or to brainstorm a new plan using Graphic Organizer 10.

Conference/Evaluate

As students draft, have them evaluate their work using the rubric on p. 104.

 Digital
- eBook
- WriteSmart
- Interactive Lessons

Short Story

A **short story** is a short piece of fiction that usually focuses on a few characters and a single event.

Parts of a Short Story

- A beginning that introduces the main characters and setting
- A middle that shows how the characters react to a problem
- Dialogue between the characters
- Colorful details that describe the events in the plot
- An ending that shows a solution to the problem

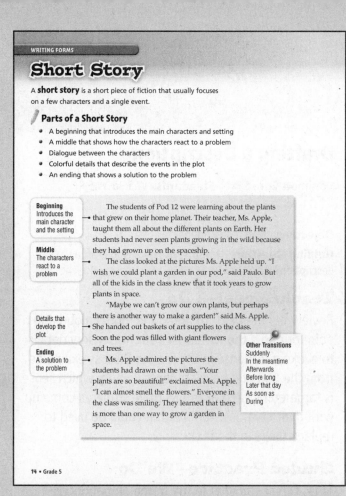

Beginning
Introduces the main character and the setting →

Middle
The characters react to a problem

Details that develop the plot →

Ending
A solution to the problem →

The students of Pod 12 were learning about the plants that grew on their home planet. Their teacher, Ms. Apple, taught them all about the different plants on Earth. Her students had never seen plants growing in the wild because they had grown up on the spaceship.

The class looked at the pictures Ms. Apple held up. "I wish we could plant a garden in our pod," said Paulo. But all of the kids in the class knew that it took years to grow plants in space.

"Maybe we can't grow our own plants, but perhaps there is another way to make a garden!" said Ms. Apple. She handed out baskets of art supplies to the class. Soon the pod was filled with giant flowers and trees.

Ms. Apple admired the pictures the students had drawn on the walls. "Your plants are so beautiful!" exclaimed Ms. Apple. "I can almost smell the flowers." Everyone in the class was smiling. They learned that there is more than one way to grow a garden in space.

Other Transitions
Suddenly
In the meantime
Afterwards
Before long
Later that day
As soon as
During

Name _____

Follow your teacher's directions to complete this page.

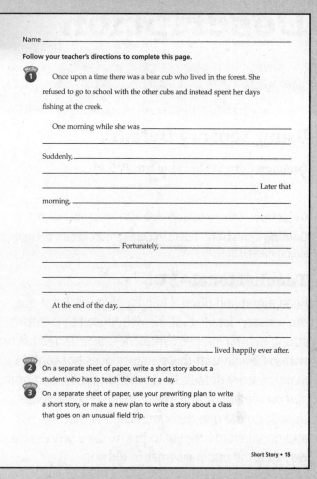

1 Once upon a time there was a bear cub who lived in the forest. She refused to go to school with the other cubs and instead spent her days fishing at the creek.

One morning while she was _____
_____
Suddenly, _____
_____
_____. Later that morning, _____
_____
_____
_____. Fortunately, _____
_____
_____
At the end of the day, _____
_____
_____
_____ lived happily ever after.

2 On a separate sheet of paper, write a short story about a student who has to teach the class for a day.

3 On a separate sheet of paper, use your prewriting plan to write a short story, or make a new plan to write a story about a class that goes on an unusual field trip.

Corrective Feedback

IF . . . students are having a hard time writing dialogue or details that show characters' reactions,

THEN . . . have them find a sentence that tells what a character does and tell them to rewrite it as something the character says. For example, *Lori told her brother that he could ask her for help* becomes *Lori said to her brother, "Don't worry, Alex. You can always come to me for help."*

Focus Trait: Ideas

Tell students that they can get ideas for stories from events in their own lives or in other people's lives. Explain that short stories usually are more interesting and authentic if the events are believable. For this reason, it is often easier to start a story with an event that happened in real life. Tell students that, to develop story ideas, writers frequently use details from real life, changing names and other details to make the story fiction. This helps readers connect to the story and stay interested in what will happen next.

Model writing the beginning of a story based on a real event in your own life, remembering to change the identity of the main character. Have students add details and dialogue to the story, imagining what they would do and say if they were the main character. Have them make a plan for how the characters will solve the problem in the story.

Description

Minilesson 3

Using Sensory Details

Common Core State Standard: W.5.3d

Objective: Choose sensory details to affect an audience.

Guiding Question: How can I use sensory details to create a strong mental image?

Teach/Model—I Do

Read aloud and discuss handbook p. 16. Point out the sensory details that the writer used to create strong mental images. Write *The sun reflected off the water.* Explain that this sentence does not contain many sensory details. Now write *The reflection of the sun on the bright blue water made tiny diamonds appear on the glassy surface.* Explain that the additional words appeal to the reader's senses in a way that the original sentence did not.

Guided Practice—We Do

On the board, write *scales, fins, gills, eyes, mouth, tail.* Tell students that together you will write a description of a fish. Help them list sensory words and phrases to describe the fish, such as *silvery scales, feathery fins,* and *eyes like copper pennies.* Then, together, sort through the items according to the sense they appeal to—sight, sound, and so on.

Practice/Apply—You Do

COLLABORATIVE Write a number of topics on the board, such as *a bird perched on a treetop, a wandering coyote,* and *a running bull.* Have groups list several sensory words and phrases to describe one of the topics. Discuss groups' lists as a class.

INDEPENDENT Have students choose another topic from the board and write sensory words and phrases about it.

Conference/Evaluate

Circulate, making sure that students are using a variety of sensory details.

Minilesson 4

Drafting a Description

Common Core State Standards: W.5.3d, W.5.8

Objective: Draft a description.

Guiding Question: How do I use details to draft a description?

Teach/Model—I Do

Review handbook p. 16. Read the model aloud and point out how the writer uses strong sensory details to evoke a response in the reader. Discuss examples from the text and have students identify which sense is targeted by each example. Have students come up with their own descriptions that could be used to replace those in the text.

Guided Practice—We Do

 Direct students to the frame on handbook p. 17. Tell them that, together, you will write a description of something that is so important to them they cannot leave home without it. Guide students to write an introductory sentence, such as *The one item I can never leave home without is my lucky pair of socks.* Work together to complete the frame. Have students write in their books as you write on the board.

Practice/Apply—You Do

 COLLABORATIVE Have groups plan and complete Activity 2. Encourage students to brainstorm strong sensory details for their paragraph.

 INDEPENDENT Have students read and follow the directions. Tell them to use their prewriting plan from Lesson 2 or to brainstorm a new plan using Graphic Organizer 5.

Conference/Evaluate

As students draft, have them evaluate their work using the rubric on p. 104.

 Digital
• eBook
• WriteSmart
• Interactive Lessons

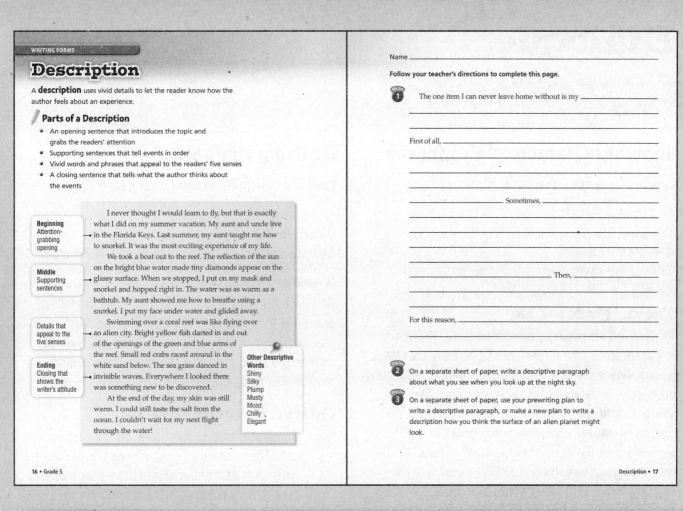

Description

A **description** uses vivid details to let the reader know how the author feels about an experience.

Parts of a Description

- An opening sentence that introduces the topic and grabs the readers' attention
- Supporting sentences that tell events in order
- Vivid words and phrases that appeal to the readers' five senses
- A closing sentence that tells what the author thinks about the events

Beginning
Attention-grabbing opening

Middle
Supporting sentences

Details that appeal to the five senses

Ending
Closing that shows the writer's attitude

I never thought I would learn to fly, but that is exactly what I did on my summer vacation. My aunt and uncle live in the Florida Keys. Last summer, my aunt taught me how to snorkel. It was the most exciting experience of my life.

We took a boat out to the reef. The reflection of the sun on the bright blue water made tiny diamonds appear on the glassy surface. When we stopped, I put on my mask and snorkel and hopped right in. The water was as warm as a bathtub. My aunt showed me how to breathe using a snorkel. I put my face under water and glided away.

Swimming over a coral reef was like flying over an alien city. Bright yellow fish darted in and out of the openings of the green and blue arms of the reef. Small red crabs raced around in the white sand below. The sea grass danced in invisible waves. Everywhere I looked there was something new to be discovered.

At the end of the day, my skin was still warm. I could still taste the salt from the ocean. I couldn't wait for my next flight through the water!

Other Descriptive Words
Shiny
Silky
Plump
Musty
Moist
Chilly
Elegant

16 • Grade 5

Name _____

Follow your teacher's directions to complete this page.

1 The one item I can never leave home without is my _____
_____

First of all, _____
_____
_____
_____
_____ Sometimes, _____
_____
_____
_____
_____ Then, _____
_____
_____
For this reason, _____
_____
_____

2 On a separate sheet of paper, write a descriptive paragraph about what you see when you look up at the night sky.

3 On a separate sheet of paper, use your prewriting plan to write a descriptive paragraph, or make a new plan to write a description how you think the surface of an alien planet might look.

Description • 17

 Corrective Feedback

IF . . . students are having a hard time coming up with sensory details that create a strong mental image,

THEN . . . tell them to think about words that describe how things taste, sound, smell, look, and feel. Encourage students to use a thesaurus if they have trouble thinking of words that evoke a strong response in readers.

Focus Trait: Voice

Explain to students that the words a writer uses to describe something often reveal the writer's attitudes and feelings toward whatever is being described. This is called the writer's voice.

The sunlight drenched the room in a warm glow.

Point out that the writer creates a warm, pleasant feeling with the details in this sentence. Then read the following sentence aloud:

The glare of the sun washed out everything in the room.

In this sentence, the sunlight is described as something unpleasant. Remind students to think about how the words they choose reflect their feelings. Guide students to come up with a few examples of their own.

Dialogue

Minilesson 5

Showing Characters' Responses

Common Core State Standard: W.5.3b

Objective: Use dialogue to show characters' responses to situations in a narrative.

Guiding Question: How can I use dialogue to show a character's feelings in a short story?

Teach/Model—I Do

Read aloud and discuss handbook p. 18. Explain that in paragraph 2, the writer doesn't just say that Isaac is annoyed. Instead, the writer uses dialogue to show how Isaac feels about his sister's actions. Ask students to discuss what each line of dialogue reveals about the character who speaks it. Tell students that dialogue should sound natural, or the way that people really talk. Practice dialogue by eliciting a few sentences from students and writing them verbatim on the board.

Guided Practice—We Do

Write *Jesse and Keisha could not agree on a name for their new kitten.* Guide students to write a few lines of dialogue to go with this scene, such as *"What about Pierre?" asked Jesse. "That's a silly name for a kitten," said Keisha.*

Practice/Apply—You Do

COLLABORATIVE Have partners write several lines of dialogue for two students who find something hidden in the classroom.

INDEPENDENT Have students write several lines of dialogue for two friends who share a secret.

Conference/Evaluate

Encourage students having difficulty writing dialogue to think about how they themselves use words to express how they feel. Explain that dialogue should express a character's feelings in the same way.

Minilesson 6

Drafting Dialogue

Common Core State Standards: W.5.3b, W.5.5

Objective: Write dialogue.

Guiding Question: How can I write realistic dialogue?

Teach/Model—I Do

Review handbook p. 18. Read aloud the model and point out how dialogue shows the characters' reactions and develops the plot. Point out how the speech the characters use sounds natural and shows their reactions to the events in the story.

Guided Practice—We Do

 Direct students to the frame on handbook p. 19. Tell them that you will work together to write part of a fictional narrative that includes dialogue showing the characters' thoughts and feelings. Help students suggest suitable dialogue, such as *Myra said, "What will happen to our class hamster, Noah?"* Have students draft the narrative in their books as you write on the board.

Practice/Apply—You Do

 COLLABORATIVE Have groups plan and complete Activity 2 about a fifth grader who gets to be President of the United States for a day. Tell students to use dialogue to show how the characters are feeling and what they are thinking. Have groups share their work.

 INDEPENDENT Have students read and follow the directions. Tell them to use their prewriting plan from Lesson 3 or to brainstorm a new plan using Graphic Organizer 11.

Conference/Evaluate

As students draft, have them evaluate their work using the rubric on p. 104.

 • eBook
• WriteSmart
• Interactive Lessons

Dialogue

Dialogue is the conversation between two or more characters in a story.

Parts of Dialogue

- Reveals a character's thoughts and feelings
- Sounds the way people talk to each other in real life
- Makes a story more lifelike and interesting
- Shows, rather than just tells, what is happening

Dialogue shows what characters think and feel →

Words sound the way people talk to each other in real life →

Details make the story interesting →

"Quiet everyone! I now call to order the meeting of all the stuffed animals from Vivian's room!" Isaac's little sister was at it again. Her toys were spread across the living room.

"Why can't you have your little meeting in your room?" Isaac grumbled. Vivian folded her arms and glared at him.

"Isaac, why don't you try playing with your little sister instead of bugging her?" His dad didn't even look up from the paper he was reading. Isaac started to complain but sat down on the floor with a sigh instead.

"Alright, Vivian. So who's the president?" Isaac asked. Vivian shrugged her shoulders. "Well, you can't have a meeting like this without a president."

Vivian looked around the room. "I know!" she yelled. "Starfox can be the president!" Their new puppy looked up excitedly at Vivian.

Isaac spent all afternoon playing with his sister. It wasn't the most fun he'd ever had, but it was better than fighting. He even smiled a little when Vivian announced, "Next, the stuffed animals go to space!"

Other Words to Describe Dialogue
Exclaimed
Wondered
Ordered
Screamed
Whispered
Pleaded
Sang
Replied

Name _____

Follow your teacher's directions to complete this page.

1 It was the last day of the school year. Myra said, "_____
_____
_____
_____
_____ "

Ms. Holiday replied, _____
_____
_____
_____

At once, the whole class smiled and exclaimed, _____
_____
_____
_____

As we left the room, Ms. Holiday said, _____
_____
_____
_____
_____

2 On a separate sheet of paper, write a story with dialogue about a kid who gets to be President of the United States for a day.

3 On a separate sheet of paper, use your prewriting plan to write a story with dialogue, or make a plan to write a new story with dialogue about someone who makes a promise he or she cannot keep.

Corrective Feedback

IF . . . students are having a hard time coming up with dialogue that is natural,

THEN . . . have them imagine a conversation before they write dialogue. When they actually write, they can use the most important parts of this imagined dialogue. Students can also read aloud their dialogue to each other to see if it sounds natural.

Focus Trait: Word Choice

Tell students that word choice is important in creating dialogue that sounds like real speech. Remind students that the words a character speaks should reflect the character's personality as well as his or her feelings. Explain that the way a teacher might express feelings about a student's work probably would be very different from the way another student would do so. Write:

"Madison, I am so proud of how well you did in the spelling bee," said Ms. Beezwax.

Then work with students to rewrite the sentence as if it were a student congratulating Madison rather than the teacher. For example:

"Way to go, Madison! You were awesome!" yelled Ethan.

Grade 5 • **19**

Fictional Narrative: Prewriting

Minilesson 7

Using a Story Map

Common Core State Standard: W.5.5

Objective: Create a story map to prewrite for a story.

Guiding Question: How can I use a story map to help me plan my story?

Teach/Model—I Do

Read aloud and discuss handbook p. 20. Explain to students that a story map is a useful tool for planning a story. Point out how the writer used a story map to identify the setting and main characters. Note that the writer also used it to plan the events that will occur at the beginning, middle, and end of the story. Demonstrate how to add characters, events, and even settings to the map, explaining that story maps make it easy to make changes or additions to a story.

Guided Practice—We Do

Draw a story map on the board. Tell students that you will do a prewrite for a story about a student who finds something unusual hidden in his desk. Write *A classroom* in the space marked *Setting.* Ask for suggestions for characters and events. Remind students that they should map out a beginning, middle, and end during the planning stage.

Practice/Apply—You Do

COLLABORATIVE Have students work in groups to fill in a story map to plan a story about a boy learning to swim. Have groups share their work.

INDEPENDENT Have students use a story map to plan a story about something unusual that happens in school.

Conference/Evaluate

Have students check to make sure that the characters, setting, and plot in their story plans fit together logically.

Minilesson 8

Planning Characters and Events

Common Core State Standard: W.5.5

Objective: Plan how the main character will change through the events of my story.

Guiding Question: How can I plan the events of my story to show how my character changes?

Teach/Model—I Do

Review handbook p. 20 with students. Explain that the descriptions of what happens at the beginning, middle, and end of the story show the problem that the main characters face and how the characters react. Review each plot point with students.

Guided Practice—We Do

 Direct students to Activity 1 on handbook p. 21. Tell students that together you will use a story map to plan a story about a boy named Jeremy who learns to swim for the first time. Remind students that their characters should face some kind of a problem in the story. Guide students through the process of creating a story map. Make sure that the map names the main characters, states the problem they face, and shows how those characters change as the events of the story take place. Have students write in their books as you write on the board.

Practice/Apply—You Do

 COLLABORATIVE Have groups plan and complete Activity 2. Tell them to use a story map to plan a story about a group of kids who form a secret club.

 INDEPENDENT Have students read and follow the directions. Remind them to include a problem for their characters to solve.

Conference/Evaluate

As students plan, have them evaluate their work using the rubric on p. 104.

 Digital
- eBook
- WriteSmart
- Interactive Lessons

Fictional Narrative: Prewriting

A **fictional narrative** is a made-up story that includes a setting, characters, and plot with a problem the characters have to solve. Prewriting is the first stage of writing in which you plan your story. One way to plan a fictional narrative is to use a story map.

Parts of Prewriting for a Fictional Narrative

- Decide on an idea for your story
- Write down the names of your characters and the setting
- Think of a problem that your characters will face in your story
- Write a short description of the events that will take place in the beginning, middle, and end of your story in your story map

Setting: The Parkers' House	**Characters:** Mrs. Parker, Charlie, Evan

Plot

Beginning
Mrs. Parker thinks Charlie and Evan are eating candy before dinner.

Middle
Charlie and Evan set up a camcorder to prove someone else is taking the candy.

End
The video shows that a squirrel is stealing the candy.

Name _____

Follow your teacher's directions to complete this page.

1

Setting	Characters

Plot

Beginning

Middle

End

2 On a separate sheet of paper, draw a story map to plan a story about a group of kids who decide to form a secret club.

3 On a separate sheet of paper, make a story map for a story about friends working together to solve a problem.

Corrective Feedback

IF . . . students have a hard time deciding how characters will change during a story,

THEN . . . remind students that characters might learn something as they face a problem. Tell students to imagine how they themselves might react and change when faced with the problem. Encourage students to use the story map to plan their story, reminding them that they can change their plan if their ideas do not work in the drafting or revising phases.

Focus Trait: Ideas

Explain to students that before they complete a story map, they should brainstorm ideas for their story. Tell students that if they get stuck and have trouble coming up with ideas for their plot, they can simply make a list of everything that comes to mind. Then they can decide which idea makes the most sense in the context of their story.

Remind students that the sequence of events in a story should be logical and believable. Explain that brainstorming can help writers decide on changes to make in a story—or even create a whole new story—if they find that they need help developing their story.

Grade 5 •

Fictional Narrative

Getting Readers Interested

Common Core State Standard: W.5.3a

Objective: Write a strong lead sentence.

Guiding Question: How can my lead sentence make people want to keep reading?

Teach/Model—I Do

Read and discuss the model on p. 22. Reread the beginning and explain that a strong beginning introduces the characters, setting, and problem; it also uses language and details that capture the readers' attention. On the board write *Delilah was a special cat.* Point out that this sentence does not engage the reader. Then write *Delilah was the fastest cat in the west,* explaining that this sentence will hook readers because it tells what makes Delilah special.

Guided Practice—We Do

Have students brainstorm five ideas for a story, such as *a dog goes on an adventure* or *two sisters find a treasure.* Guide students to choose one. Work with students to write a strong beginning for one of the topics.

Practice/Apply—You Do

COLLABORATIVE Have groups choose two more topics from the list on the board and write a strong beginning for each.

INDEPENDENT Have students write a strong beginning for one of the remaining topics. Remind them that their opening sentence should hook their readers.

Conference/Evaluate

Encourage students having trouble writing a strong beginning to orally present several options to a peer. Then, before they write, they can work together to make sure that their beginning sentences capture readers' attention with an interesting fact or surprising [word] and phrases.

Drafting a Fictional Narrative

Common Core State Standard: W.5.3c

Objective: Write a fictional narrative in chronological order.

Guiding Question: In what order should the events in my story happen?

Teach/Model—I Do

Review handbook p. 22 with students. Point out that the beginning introduces the main characters and places them in a situation that gets the plot rolling. In the body of the story, events unfold in logical order. Point out how time-order transition words help show the sequence of events in the model. Discuss how dialogue shows what the characters are like and tells part of the story.

Guided Practice—We Do

 Direct students to the frame on handbook p. 23. Guide them to use their plans from the previous lesson to write a story about a boy learning to swim. Work together to put the information from the story map into a story, with a strong opening and dialogue. For example, *He had never swum before and was terrified of getting in the pool.* Help students create sentences to complete the frame. Have students write in their books as you write on the board.

Practice/Apply—You Do

 COLLABORATIVE Have groups complete Activity 2 about friends who solve a mystery. Have groups share their work.

 INDEPENDENT Have students read and follow the directions. Tell them to use their prewriting plan from the previous lesson or make a new plan for a fictional narrative.

Conference/Evaluate

As students draft, have them evaluate their work using the rubric on p. 104.

 Digital
- eBook
- WriteSmart
- Interactive Lessons

Fictional Narrative

A **fictional narrative** is a made-up story about characters solving a problem, or conflict.

Parts of a Fictional Narrative

- A beginning introducing the characters, setting, and problem
- A middle that shows the personalities of the characters and the actions they take toward solving a problem
- Events told in a logical order
- Dialogue that gives each character a unique voice
- An ending that shows how the problem is solved

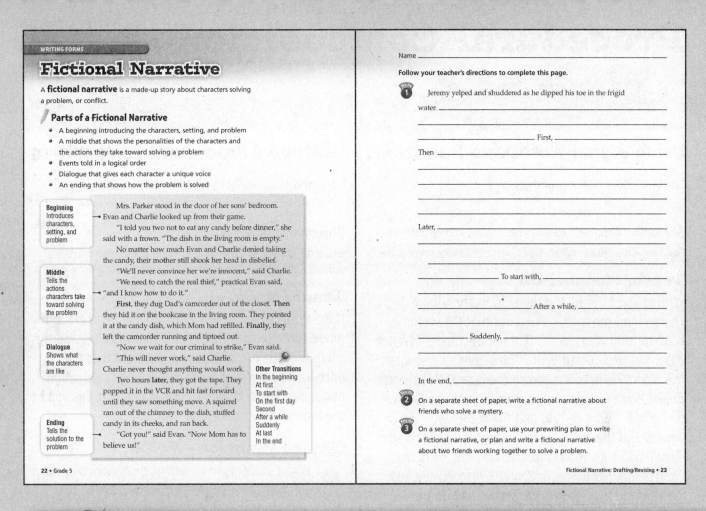

Beginning Introduces characters, setting, and problem

Mrs. Parker stood in the door of her sons' bedroom. Evan and Charlie looked up from their game.

"I told you two not to eat any candy before dinner," she said with a frown. "The dish in the living room is empty."

No matter how much Evan and Charlie denied taking the candy, their mother still shook her head in disbelief.

"We'll never convince her we're innocent," said Charlie.

"We need to catch the real thief," practical Evan said, "and I know how to do it."

Middle Tells the actions characters take toward solving the problem

First, they dug Dad's camcorder out of the closet. **Then** they hid it on the bookcase in the living room. They pointed it at the candy dish, which Mom had refilled. **Finally**, they left the camcorder running and tiptoed out.

"Now we wait for our criminal to strike," Evan said.

Dialogue Shows what the characters are like

"This will never work," said Charlie.

Charlie never thought anything would work.

Two hours **later**, they got the tape. They popped it in the VCR and hit fast forward until they saw something move. A squirrel ran out of the chimney to the dish, stuffed candy in its cheeks, and ran back.

Ending Tells the solution to the problem

"Got you!" said Evan. "Now Mom has to believe us!"

Other Transitions
In the beginning
At first
To start with
On the first day
Second
After a while
Suddenly
At last
In the end

22 • Grade 5

Name _____

Follow your teacher's directions to complete this page.

1 Jeremy yelped and shuddered as he dipped his toe in the frigid water. _____

_____ First, _____

Then _____

_____

_____

_____

_____

Later, _____

_____

_____

_____ To start with, _____

_____

_____ After a while, _____

_____

_____ Suddenly, _____

In the end, _____

2 On a separate sheet of paper, write a fictional narrative about friends who solve a mystery.

3 On a separate sheet of paper, use your prewriting plan to write a fictional narrative, or plan and write a fictional narrative about two friends working together to solve a problem.

✔ Corrective Feedback

IF . . . students are having difficulty showing the time relationship between the events in their story,

THEN . . . direct them to the list of Other Transitions in the model. Have students create their own lists of words they can use to show when the events of the story took place.

Focus Trait: Voice

Explain to students that voice refers to how a writer's attitude comes through the language he or she uses.

Katie was an active puppy.

Explain that, in this sentence, the writer uses the word *active* to describe the puppy. Point out that this is a neutral word that doesn't express any real feeling or attitude about the puppy.

Next, write the following on the board:

Katie was a frisky, playful puppy.

Point out that the words *frisky* and *playful* show a positive feeling toward the puppy.

Remind students that the words they choose will create a voice and that they should choose words consistently so that the voice is clear.

Procedural Composition

| Minilesson 11 | Minilesson 12 |

Using Signal Words and Transitions

Common Core State Standard: W.5.2c

Objective: Describe a step-by-step process in time order.

Guiding Question: What words can I use to show time order?

Teach/Model—I Do

With students, read and then discuss handbook p. 24. Then reread the model. Point out that the words in bold are transition words that tell the reader in what order the steps occur. Write *The carpenter measures the wood. He marks a line on the board. He saws the board.* Point out that these steps do not have transition words. To be certain that the reader will understand the order in which things happen, writers should add transition words. Write *First, Next,* and *Then* before Sentences 1, 2, and 3 respectively. To indicate the final step, add a sentence with the appropriate transition word, such as *Finally, he smooths the edge with sandpaper.*

Guided Practice—We Do

Tell students that you will work together to explain the steps cooks follow to make a tuna salad sandwich. Help them identify the steps needed and then place them in the correct order. Help students suggest time-order transition words to use. Write their suggestions on the board.

Practice/Apply—You Do

COLLABORATIVE Write a number of familiar topics on the board, such as *build a sand castle, shoot a basketball,* and *find a book in the library.* Have small groups choose a task, explain the steps, and include transition words.

INDEPENDENT Have students choose another topic, explain the steps, and include transition words.

Conference/Evaluate

Encourage students who are having trouble to explain their procedure to a partner before they write. They should then see if the partner understands the process.

Drafting a Procedural Composition

Common Core State Standards: W.5.2

Objective: Write instructions.

Guiding Question: In what order do I place the steps in a process so readers can understand them?

Teach/Model—I Do

Have students review handbook p. 24. Read aloud the model, pointing out the boldfaced transitions and the list in the Other Transitions box. Explain that the introduction begins with an interesting observation about panning and then clearly states that this will be the topic of the essay.

Guided Practice—We Do

 Direct students to the frame on handbook p. 25. Tell them to suppose they are explaining to a new student how they usually start the day. Read the first sentence and point out the transitions. Guide students to suggest things a teacher does at the beginning of the day, the order in which he or she does them, and transition words to show the order. List the suggestions on the board. Help students use the ideas from the list to complete the frame. Have students write in their books as you write on the board.

Practice/Apply—You Do

 COLLABORATIVE Have small groups plan and complete the activity. Have groups share and discuss what they have written.

 INDEPENDENT Have students read and follow the directions. Tell them to use their prewriting plan from Lesson 6 or to brainstorm a new plan using Graphic Organizer 4.

Conference/Evaluate

As students draft, circulate and help them choose transition words that place steps in order. Evaluate using the rubric on p. 104.

 Digital
- eBook
- WriteSmart
- Interactive Lessons

Procedural Composition

A **procedural composition** explains a procedure, or step-by-step process, for doing something. It is written in time order, or sequence.

Parts of a Procedural Composition

* An introduction that tells what the essay will explain
* A body that gives the sequence of steps or events that make up the procedure
* Transition words that tell the order of the steps or events
* A conclusion that restates the topic and makes a final comment

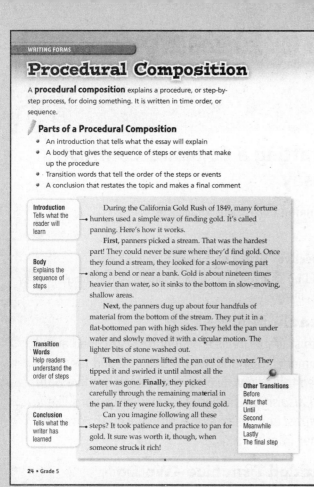

Introduction
Tells what the reader will learn

During the California Gold Rush of 1849, many fortune hunters used a simple way of finding gold. It's called panning. Here's how it works.

Body
Explains the sequence of steps

First, panners picked a stream. That was the hardest part! They could never be sure where they'd find gold. Once they found a stream, they looked for a slow-moving part along a bend or near a bank. Gold is about nineteen times heavier than water, so it sinks to the bottom in slow-moving, shallow areas.

Next, the panners dug up about four handfuls of material from the bottom of the stream. They put it in a flat-bottomed pan with high sides. They held the pan under water and slowly moved it with a circular motion. The lighter bits of stone washed out.

Transition Words
Help readers understand the order of steps

Then the panners lifted the pan out of the water. They tipped it and swirled it until almost all the water was gone. **Finally**, they picked carefully through the remaining material in the pan. If they were lucky, they found gold.

Other Transitions
Before
After that
Until
Second
Meanwhile
Lastly
The final step

Conclusion
Tells what the writer has learned

Can you imagine following all these steps? It took patience and practice to pan for gold. It sure was worth it, though, when someone struck it rich!

Name _____

Follow your teacher's directions to complete this page.

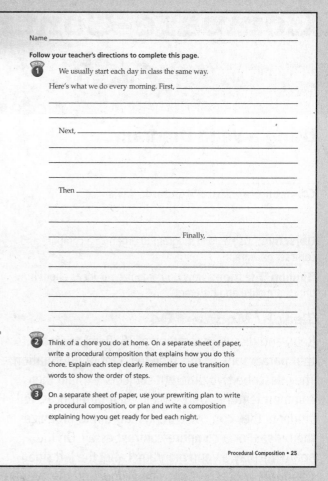

1 We usually start each day in class the same way.

Here's what we do every morning. First, _____

_____

_____

Next, _____

_____

_____

_____

Then _____

_____

_____

_____ Finally, _____

_____

_____

_____

_____

_____

2 Think of a chore you do at home. On a separate sheet of paper, write a procedural composition that explains how you do this chore. Explain each step clearly. Remember to use transition words to show the order of steps.

3 On a separate sheet of paper, use your prewriting plan to write a procedural composition, or plan and write a composition explaining how you get ready for bed each night.

Corrective Feedback

IF . . . students are having difficulty putting steps in order,

THEN . . . have them use a flow chart to brainstorm a sequence of events. They can write each step in a box, beginning at the top for the first step and following the arrow down the page to the next step in the sequence. Remind students that, when they begin to write, adding time-order or transition words to sentences can help readers understand the order of the ideas, or steps.

Focus Trait: Organization

Explain to students that they can use a word-processing program to help organize the sequence of steps in a procedure. Tell them to open a new file and type each step on a separate line. The steps don't have to be in order at first. To move a line to a better place in the sequence, select it and drag it to the new position. Continue until each step is in the correct order.

Type this example on a computer:

I poured the milk.
I got out a bowl.
I poured cereal into the bowl.

Elicit from students how the sequence can be revised. Select and drag the steps into a new order:

I got out a bowl.
I poured cereal into the bowl.
I poured the milk.

Compare-Contrast Essay

Minilesson 13

Using a Venn Diagram

Common Core State Standard: W.5.5

Objective: Use a Venn diagram to organize a compare and contrast paragraph.

Guiding Question: How do I organize my ideas about how things are alike and different?

Teach/Model—I Do

Read and discuss handbook p. 26. Remind students that paragraphs of this type tell a lot of information. They describe two different subjects, explain their common features, and explain their differences. Tell students they can use a Venn diagram to organize their ideas for a compare-contrast essay. On the board, display a Venn diagram. Label the left side *Charlotte*. Label the right side *Wilbur* and the overlap *Both*. Then read the paragraph. Explain that the ways the kittens are alike go in the overlap. Write in the overlap *kittens, gray, white paws, white tail tips*. Finish filling in the outer circles of the diagram with parallel details that tell how the two kittens differ.

Guided Practice—We Do

Write a list of topic pairs on the board, such as *two friends, apples and oranges*, and *bicycles and cars*. Display an empty Venn diagram on chart paper. Together, choose one pair and list similarities and differences. Fill in the diagram, and save it for use in Minilesson 14.

Practice/Apply—You Do

COLLABORATIVE Have groups choose another pair from the list. Tell them to fill in a Venn diagram with ideas about the topic. Have them save their work.

INDEPENDENT Have students fill in a Venn diagram for another pair from the board or a new pair.

Conference/Evaluate

Make sure students are setting up their Venn diagrams correctly. Remind them that similarities go in the middle and differences go on the outside.

Minilesson 14

Drafting a Compare-Contrast Essay

Common Core State Standards: W.5.2a, W.5.2c, W.5.2e

Objective: Write a compare-and-contrast essay.

Guiding Question: How can I show how two things are alike and different?

Teach/Model—I Do

With students, review handbook p. 26. Read aloud the model, pointing out the subjects and the bold-faced transitions. Explain that transitions like *both* and *also* signal similarities, while transitions like *in contrast* and *unlike* signal differences. Go over the Other Transitions list.

Guided Practice—We Do

 Direct students to the frame on handbook p. 27. Post the Venn diagram you created with the class for the We Do section in Minilesson 13. Help students use the ideas in the diagram to complete the frame, beginning with similarities and ending with differences. Have students write in their books as you write on the board.

Practice/Apply—You Do

 COLLABORATIVE Have small groups complete Activity 2, using the ideas in the Venn diagram that they created collaboratively for Minilesson 13. Have groups share and discuss what they have written.

 INDEPENDENT Have students complete the activity. Tell them to use their prewriting plan from Lesson 7 or to brainstorm a new plan using Graphic Organizer 14.

Conference/Evaluate

As students draft, circulate and help them choose similarities and differences. Evaluate using the rubric on p. 104.

 Digital
- Compare-Contrast Essay;
- Transitions

Compare-Contrast Essay

A **compare-contrast essay** shows how two people, places, or things are alike and how they are different.

Parts of a Compare-Contrast Essay

- An introduction that tells who or what is being compared and contrasted
- A body that is organized logically: similarities first, then differences; differences, then similarities; or similarities and differences point by point
- Vivid details that make similarities and differences clear
- A conclusion that summarizes or makes a final comment

Introduction
Tells who is being compared and contrasted

Body
Lists similarities, then differences

Vivid Details
Make points clear

Conclusion
Summarizes and comments

It is hard to believe that my kittens, Wilbur and Charlotte, can look so alike but be so different.

Both kittens are light gray and have white paws. **Also,** each cat has a long, bushy tail with a bright white tip.

That is pretty much where the similarities end, however. For one thing, Charlotte loves to be out and about, and she is always getting into trouble. When I am reading, she sneaks over and tries to grab the pages as I turn them. She even got into my parents' closet and pulled down all my father's ties. She has quite an appetite, too. She is always as hungry as a wolf! She keeps following me around until I give in and put some food in her bowl. **In contrast,** Wilbur never causes trouble. He is so shy that he is always off somewhere by himself. We even found him hiding on top of the refrigerator one day! **Unlike** Charlotte, Wilbur always waits patiently to be fed.

All in all, no one would ever think that these two cats are brother and sister. Still, even though Wilbur and Charlotte are so different, everyone in our family loves them equally.

Other Transitions
Another
As well
Likewise
But
However
Finally

Name _____

Follow your teacher's directions to complete this page.

 1 _____
_____
_____
_____
Both _____
_____
_____
_____ Also, _____
_____ In contrast, _____
_____
_____
_____ Unlike _____
_____ All in all, _____
_____
_____

 2 On a separate sheet of paper, plan and write a compare-contrast essay describing two kinds of animals.

3 On a separate sheet of paper, use your prewriting plan to write a compare-contrast essay, or make a plan and write to compare and contrast two characters in a book you like.

✔ Corrective Feedback

IF . . . students are unable to come up with at least one similarity and difference for two people or story characters,

THEN . . . have them write a list of qualities they would use to describe, such as *appearance*, *personality*, *age*, and so on. Then have them fill out the list for each character or person and make point-to-point comparisons.

Focus Trait: Word Choice

Remind students that they should use linking words and transitions to show similarities and differences.

On the board, write a few sentences comparing and contrasting characters from a story the class has read, leaving out the transition words. For example:

Dorothy needs to get home. The Scarecrow just wants a brain. They ask the Wizard for help.

Work with students to rewrite the sentences, adding transition and linking words to help show similarities and differences. Underline these words as you write.

Dorothy needs to get home, <u>but</u> the Scarecrow just wants a brain. They <u>both</u> ask the Wizard for help.

Cause and Effect Essay

Minilesson 15

Prewriting for Cause and Effect

Common Core State Standard: W.5.2

Objective: Identify a cause and its effect.
Guiding Question: Which events lead to other events?

Teach/Model—I Do

Read aloud and discuss handbook p. 28. Point out the cause-and-effect relationships in sentences 5–8 of the model. Tell students that, when they prewrite, they should figure out which events cause others to happen. Write *When the door slammed, Patty screamed.* Explain that two events happened: the door slammed, and Patty screamed. Model identifying which event is the cause and which event is the effect. For example, *Patty must have been scared if she screamed. The door probably startled her, making her scream.* The door slammed *must be the cause and* Patty screamed *must be the effect.* Tell students that filling in a cause-and-effect T-Map (Graphic Organizer 13) can help them identify causes and effects. Also point out that some causes may have more than one effect.

Guided Practice—We Do

Write a number of events on the board, such as *heavy rainfall, baby brother or sister is born,* and *moving to a new place to live.* Together, pick one cause and brainstorm possible effects. Remind students that some effects may lead to other effects.

Practice/Apply—You Do

COLLABORATIVE Have small groups choose another cause from the board and write one or two effects for it.

INDEPENDENT Have students choose a new cause from the board and write one effect.

Conference/Evaluate

Circulate and help students list words that show cause and effect, such as *because* or *as a result.*

Minilesson 16

Drafting a Cause and Effect Essay

Common Core State Standards: W.5.2a, W.5.2c

Objective: Draft a cause-and-effect essay.
Guiding Question: How can I show cause and effect?

Teach/Model—I Do

Have students review the definition and Parts of a Cause and Effect Essay on handbook p. 28. Read aloud the model, pointing out the transition words that help show cause-and-effect relationships. Point out the other transition words.

Guided Practice—We Do

 Direct students to the frame on handbook p. 29. Point out the topic sentence and transitions. Guide students to suggest possible effects of recycling paper, such as *forests will be able to keep growing.* List the suggestions on the board. Help students use the list to complete the frame. Have students write in their books as you write on the board.

Practice/Apply—You Do

 COLLABORATIVE Have small groups complete Activity 2. Remind groups they can use a graphic organizer to plan. Have them share and discuss what they have written.

 INDEPENDENT Have students read the directions. Tell them to use their prewriting plan from Lesson 8 or to brainstorm a new plan, using Graphic Organizer 13.

Conference/Evaluate

As students draft, help them choose words that show cause-and-effect relationships. Evaluate using the rubric on p. 104.

 • Cause-and-Effect Essay

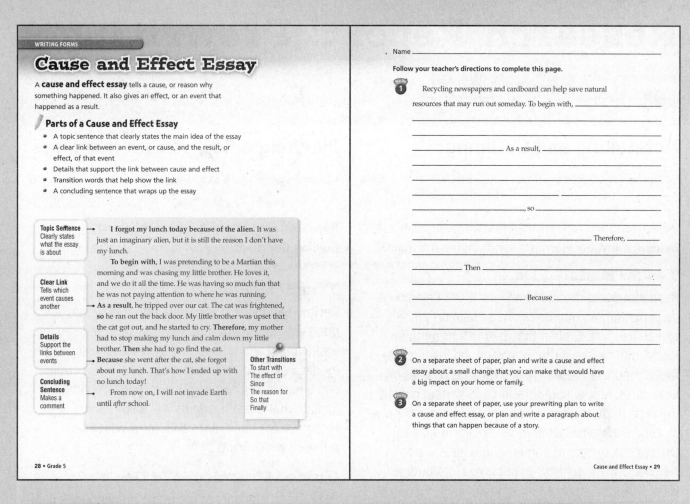

Cause and Effect Essay

A **cause and effect essay** tells a cause, or reason why something happened. It also gives an effect, or an event that happened as a result.

Parts of a Cause and Effect Essay

- A topic sentence that clearly states the main idea of the essay
- A clear link between an event, or cause, and the result, or effect, of that event
- Details that support the link between cause and effect
- Transition words that help show the link
- A concluding sentence that wraps up the essay

Topic Sentence Clearly states what the essay is about	**I forgot my lunch today because of the alien.** It was just an imaginary alien, but it is still the reason I don't have my lunch.
Clear Link Tells which event causes another	**To begin with**, I was pretending to be a Martian this morning and was chasing my little brother. He loves it, and we do it all the time. He was having so much fun that he was not paying attention to where he was running. **As a result**, he tripped over our cat. The cat was frightened, **so** he ran out the back door. My little brother was upset that the cat got out, and he started to cry. **Therefore**, my mother had to stop making my lunch and calm down my little brother. **Then** she had to go find the cat.
Details Support the links between events	
Concluding Sentence Makes a comment	**Because** she went after the cat, she forgot about my lunch. That's how I ended up with no lunch today! From now on, I will not invade Earth until *after* school.

Other Transitions
To start with
The effect of
Since
The reason for
So that
Finally

Name _____

Follow your teacher's directions to complete this page.

1 Recycling newspapers and cardboard can help save natural resources that may run out someday. To begin with, _____

_____

_____

_____ As a result, _____

_____

_____

_____ , so _____

_____

_____ Therefore, _____

_____ Then _____

_____

_____ Because _____

_____

_____

_____

2 On a separate sheet of paper, plan and write a cause and effect essay about a small change that you can make that would have a big impact on your home or family.

3 On a separate sheet of paper, use your prewriting plan to write a cause and effect essay, or plan and write a paragraph about things that can happen because of a story.

Corrective Feedback

IF . . . students are unable to come up with a cause-and-effect relationship between events,

THEN . . . have them write their ideas in a T-Map, such as Graphic Organizer 13. They should put the first thing that happened in the left column, with events that happened later in the right column. Have them reread the list to see which events in the right column were caused by the event in the left column.

Focus Trait: Ideas

Tell students that, before they write, they should brainstorm ideas that will interest readers. One way to start is to think about questions they would like to find the answers to, such as *Why do some cities have more people than others?* or *Why are basketball players so tall?*

Have students make a list of questions like these. Then have them use classroom resources such as books or the Internet to research the answer to those questions.

Once students have a few details, they should fill out a T-Map to show cause-and-effect relationships between the answers they found and their questions.

Research Report: Prewriting

Minilesson 17

Notetaking and Outlining

Common Core State Standards: W.5.5, W.5.8

Objective: Select appropriate information and organize it.

Guiding Question: How do I organize my research report?

Teach/Model—I Do

Read aloud and discuss handbook p. 30. Remind students that an outline can help them organize a research report. Explain that, before writing the model outline, the writer brainstormed ideas, chose a topic, conducted research, and recorded details on note cards. Model paraphrasing and writing notes for the facts in the second paragraph, such as *first game in 1967* and *games used to take place in January.* Discuss the system of numerals and letters used in outlines and model how to put notes into outline form.

Guided Practice—We Do

With students, brainstorm a topic for a research report, such as *George Washington.* Help students use a classroom resource such as a textbook or the Internet to find a few facts and take notes. Together, organize the notes into an outline.

Practice/Apply—You Do

COLLABORATIVE Have small groups use their social studies text to find information and take notes about another historical figure they have studied. Tell them to organize the notes into an outline. Have groups share what they have written.

INDEPENDENT Have students repeat the above activity for another research topic they have studied in science class.

Conference/Evaluate

Encourage students having trouble researching to think of the 5 Ws + H: *Who, What, When, Where, Why, + How.* Explain that answering these questions will help them find important facts.

Minilesson 18

Planning a Report with Headings

Common Core State Standards: W.5.5, W.5.8

Objective: Plan a research report with headings.

Guiding Question: How do I plan a research report with headings?

Teach/Model—I Do

Review handbook p. 30. Explain that headings are a good way to organize information so that it can be easily found and understood by readers. Discuss the model. Point out that each main idea in the outline can be used as a heading in a research report. Explain that these headings will help readers recognize the main ideas and know which facts relate to which ideas.

Guided Practice—We Do

 Direct students to the frame on handbook p. 31. Tell them that, together, you will plan a research report about the history of your state. Provide students with access to research materials, such as books and the Internet, and guide them to choose facts to list under each heading, such as *The Spanish and French were the first Europeans to settle in Florida.* Have students write in their books as you write on the board.

Practice/Apply—You Do

 COLLABORATIVE Have groups plan and complete Activity 2. Tell them to create an outline for a research report about the history of a favorite sport or game. Have groups share their work with the class.

 INDEPENDENT Have students read and follow the directions. Tell them they can use the notes they made for Minilesson 17 or to brainstorm a new topic.

Conference/Evaluate

As students draft, have them evaluate their work using the rubric on p. 104.

Digital
• eBook
• WriteSmart
• Interactive Lessons

Research Report: Prewriting

A **research report** is a nonfiction composition that uses facts gathered from several sources of information to tell about a topic. One way to plan a research report is to make an outline.

Parts of Prewriting for a Research Report

- Brainstorm ideas for your research report
- Decide on a main topic and write your thesis statement
- Research your topic and record important details on note cards
- Organize the details from your note cards into an outline that will guide you when you write your report
- Check to see that all of the details you included in your outline support your thesis

I. Introduction: The Super Bowl
    A. Exciting game
    B. Most watched sport on TV

II. History of the Super Bowl
    A. First game in 1967
    B. Originally called the AFL-NFL Championship Game
    C. Games took place in January until 2004

III. Super Bowl Records
    A. Miami Dolphins the only team to have undefeated season (Super Bowl VII)
    B. Pittsburg Steelers first team to win six Super Bowls (2009)

IV. Conclusion
    A. Winners are the best team in the world
    B. Interesting things always happen
    C. 111 million people watched the Super Bowl in 2011

Name _____

Follow your teacher's directions to complete this page.

I. Introduction: _____
    A. _____
    B. _____
    C. _____

II. First Settlers
    A. _____
    B. _____
    C. _____

III. Important Historical Events
    A. _____
    B. _____
    C. _____

IV. Conclusion
    A. _____
    B. _____
    C. _____

2 On a separate sheet of paper, prewrite for a research report about the history of your favorite sport or game. Create an outline to use as a guide for writing the report.

3 On a separate sheet of paper, prewrite for a research report on a science or social studies topic of your choice. Create an outline to use as a guide for writing the report.

Corrective Feedback

IF . . . students are having a hard time coming up with outline headings for their research reports,

THEN . . . have them group related details together. Then have them ask themselves how the details are similar. The response to this question should lead them to a heading.

Focus Trait: Ideas

Tell students that they can use a variety of resources to get ideas for their research reports. Encourage them to use more than one source when finding information for a research report, explaining that this will help them get a more balanced perspective on their topic.

Allow students time to research their topics. If necessary, remind them how to search periodicals, use encyclopedias, and locate books about their topic. Explain to students that the Internet often can be a good research tool. Point out that, unfortunately, it is more difficult to verify information found online. Show students how to search for information within a specific domain (i.e. *.edu* for information found within a university domain and *.gov* for information found on a government website). Emphasize that information from a recognized authority—a college or university, a government agency, or a respected expert—usually can be trusted.

Research Report

Minilesson 19	**Minilesson 20**

Writing a Strong Conclusion

Common Core State Standard: W.5.2.e

Objective: Write a strong conclusion for my research report.

Guiding Question: How do I write a strong conclusion for my research report?

Teach/Model—I Do

Read aloud and discuss handbook p. 32. Reread the last paragraph of the model to students. Explain that the conclusion is the last thing that readers read and that it leaves a strong impression in their minds. Point out how the conclusion of the model summarizes key ideas and wraps up the main points. Note, too, how the writer saved an interesting fact for the conclusion.

Guided Practice—We Do

Revisit the outline about the history of your state from Lesson 9. Work with students to use the Conclusion section of the outline to draft a conclusion paragraph. Guide them to summarize the key points in their outline and to leave a strong impression in the reader's mind.

Practice/Apply—You Do

COLLABORATIVE Have small groups repeat the activity with a different outline from the previous lesson or something else they have worked on in class.

INDEPENDENT Have students repeat the above activity for another outline or choose a new topic and write a concluding paragraph about it.

Conference/Evaluate

Encourage any students having trouble coming up with a strong conclusion to think about their main ideas and any details that might be particularly interesting to a reader. Remind students that the conclusion is the last thing that readers will see and that it will leave the strongest impression on them.

Drafting a Research Report

Common Core State Standards: W.5.5, W.5.6

Objective: Write a draft of a research report.

Guiding Question: How do I write a report?

Teach/Model—I Do

Review handbook p. 32. Explain that in their reports, writers must credit each fact in order to avoid plagiarism. Remind students that plagiarism is using someone else's facts or ideas without giving credit. Explain that credit should be given regardless of whether the facts are paraphrased or quoted word for word. Review the model, and point out how the writer credits sources.

Guided Practice—We Do

 Direct students to the frame on handbook p. 33. Using the outline you made in Lesson 9, complete the frame with facts about Florida. Write a credit for the source, either in a sentence or as a citation in parentheses. For example, *Florida became a major tourist destination after World War II (Roberts, 16)*. Have students write in their books as you write on the board.

Practice/Apply—You Do

 COLLABORATIVE Have groups use their outlines from the Collaborative section of the previous lesson to plan and complete Activity 2. Have groups share their work.

 INDEPENDENT Have students read and follow the directions. Tell them to use their prewriting plan from the previous lesson or to brainstorm a new plan using an outline.

Conference/Evaluate

As students draft, have them evaluate their work using the rubric on p. 104.

 Digital
- eBook
- WriteSmart
- Interactive Lessons

Research Report

A **research report** is a nonfiction composition that uses facts gathered from several sources of information to tell about a topic.

Parts of a Research Report

- An introductory paragraph that tells what the report is about
- Body paragraphs with main ideas supported by facts, details, and examples gathered from different sources
- A concluding paragraph that briefly restates or summarizes the information in the report

Introductory Paragraph Tells what the report is about	The Super Bowl is the championship of the National Football League. More people watch the Super Bowl on TV than any other sports event in the United States.
Body Paragraphs Use facts and details to support each main idea	There are many interesting facts in Super Bowl history. The first game, in 1967, was not called the Super Bowl. It was called the AFL-NFL World Championship Game (Karlis 45). Mac Hartley's book *A Football Century* says Kansas City Chiefs owner Lamar Hunt came up with the new name. He got the idea when he saw his kids playing with what they called a "super ball." **Also**, the games used to
Information Source Tells where paraphrased information was found	take place in January. Since 2004, however, they have been held in February (Hazell 176).
	Many records have been set at the Super Bowl. **For example**, the Miami Dolphins
Examples Support the main ideas	became the only team in NFL history to have an undefeated season when they beat the Washington Redskins in Super Bowl VII (Karlis 67). **In addition**, in February 2009, the Pittsburgh Steelers became the first team to win six Super Bowls (89).
Concluding Paragraph Summarizes the report	It is not hard to see why the Super Bowl is so popular. Teams always play hard. The winners can say they are the best team in the world. Interesting things often happen, as well. Perhaps that is why 111 million people watched Super Bowl XLV in 2011!

Other Transitions
Second
Another
So
For instance
Finally
In conclusion

Name _____

Follow your teacher's directions to complete this page.

1 Since its founding in 1559, Florida has had a rich history. Today it is still an interesting place to live. There is a lot you can learn about Florida!

_____

_____

_____ Also _____

_____

_____

_____

_____

_____

_____ For example, _____

_____

_____ In addition, _____

_____

_____

_____

2 On a separate sheet of paper, write a research report about a sport you like to watch or play. Use at least two sources to find interesting facts and details to include in your report.

3 On a separate sheet of paper, use your prewriting plan to write a research report, or plan and write a new report about a social studies or science topic of your choice. Use your textbook as one source of information.

Corrective Feedback

IF . . . students are having difficulty deciding which facts they need to cite in a research report,

THEN . . . explain that any fact or idea learned from a source should be noted. Point out that writers need not give a citation for a well-known fact *(The world is round; Cows give milk)* but that more specific facts (such as *Holsteins are prized dairy cows)* should be cited. Review how the writer gave credit to sources in the model. Explain to students that they can cite sources within the text of their report or on a separate Works Cited page. Model how to create a Works Cited page.

Focus Trait: Sentence Fluency

Explain to students that the sentences in their report should flow together easily. Tell them that they should use a variety of sentence structures and sentence lengths to make their reports interesting to read.

The first Super Bowl game took place in 1967. It was not called the Super Bowl. It was called the AFL-NFL World Championship Game.

Explain to students that these three sentences are each grammatically correct, but when read together the text is choppy and boring. Copy the following passage from the model on the board:

The first game, in 1967, was not called the Super Bowl. It was called the AFL-NFL World Championship Game.

Explain to students that these two sentences contain the same facts as the first three, but they are presented in a way that flows together smoothly.

Opinion Essay

Minilesson 21

Facts and Opinions

Common Core State Standard: W.5.1a

Objective: Write an opinion statement.

Guiding Question: What makes a topic sentence an opinion statement?

Teach/Model—I Do

With students, read and discuss the definition, Parts of an Opinion Essay, and model on p. 34. Explain that an opinion statement tells what the writer thinks about a topic. Write *1. All students should have the right to be heard. 2. Each student council member serves for one school year.* Emphasize that sentence 1 is an opinion, but sentence 2 is a fact.

Guided Practice—We Do

On the board write *1. All the choices on the school lunch menu are excellent. 2. Every Monday we have pizza for lunch.* Help students determine which sentence states an opinion (*1*), which sentence states a fact (*2*), and which words indicate an opinion (*All, are excellent*). Help students turn sentence 2 into an opinion.

Practice/Apply—You Do

COLLABORATIVE Write *1. Many students play team sports. 2. Soccer is the best team sport.* Have small groups repeat the three steps under Guided Practice and then share and discuss their work.

INDEPENDENT Write *1. Fifth-graders put on a play each year. 2. Everyone loves being in a play.* Have students repeat the steps used in Guided Practice and discuss their work as a class.

Conference/Evaluate

Help students having trouble by discussing words and phrases that show opinions.

Minilesson 22

Drafting an Opinion Essay

Common Core State Standard: W.5.1

Objective: Draft an opinion essay..

Guiding Question: How can I convince my audience to agree with my opinion?

Teach/Model—I Do

Discuss the model on p. 34. Point out the opinion statement and the reasons that support the opinion. Remind students that an opinion essay uses facts to support opinions. Review the transitions in the Other Transitions box.

Guided Practice—We Do

 Direct students to the frame on handbook p. 35. Tell them that, together, you will write an opinion essay about a cause for which your class should raise money. Work together to choose a topic, such as donating to an animal shelter. Help students come up with a list of reasons to support their opinions, such as *First of all, the animal shelter always needs food.* Remind students that the final sentence should restate the original opinion statement in new words. Have students write in their books as you write on the board.

Practice/Apply—You Do

 COLLABORATIVE Have groups plan and complete Activity 2. Suggest classroom rules that students might write about. Have groups share and discuss their work.

 INDEPENDENT Have students read and follow the directions. Tell them to use their prewriting plan from Lesson 11 or to brainstorm a new plan using Graphic Organizer 7.

Conference/Evaluate

As students draft, have them evaluate their work using the rubric on p. 104.

- eBook
- WriteSmart
- Interactive Lessons

Opinion Essay

An **opinion essay** tells what the writer thinks about a topic. It also explains why the writer has this view.

Parts of an Opinion Essay

- An introduction with a clearly stated opinion
- A body with reasons to support the opinion
- Facts and examples to support the main points
- Organization that is clear and logical
- A conclusion that restates the opinion

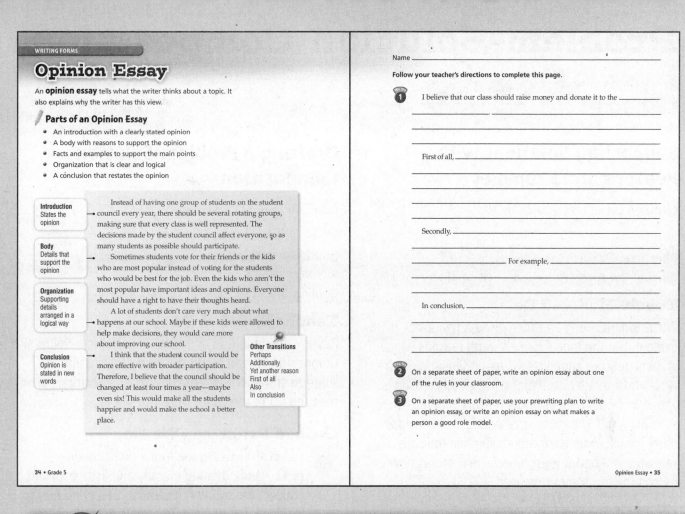

Introduction
States the opinion

Body
Details that support the opinion

Organization
Supporting details arranged in a logical way

Conclusion
Opinion is stated in new words

Instead of having one group of students on the student council every year, there should be several rotating groups, making sure that every class is well represented. The decisions made by the student council affect everyone, so as many students as possible should participate.

Sometimes students vote for their friends or the kids who are most popular instead of voting for the students who would be best for the job. Even the kids who aren't the most popular have important ideas and opinions. Everyone should have a right to have their thoughts heard.

A lot of students don't care very much about what happens at our school. Maybe if these kids were allowed to help make decisions, they would care more about improving our school.

I think that the student council would be more effective with broader participation. Therefore, I believe that the council should be changed at least four times a year—maybe even six! This would make all the students happier and would make the school a better place.

Other Transitions
Perhaps
Additionally
Yet another reason
First of all
Also
In conclusion

Name _____

Follow your teacher's directions to complete this page.

1 I believe that our class should raise money and donate it to the _____

_____ _____

_____

First of all, _____

_____

_____

_____

Secondly, _____

_____

_____ For example, _____

_____

_____

In conclusion, _____

_____

_____

_____

2 On a separate sheet of paper, write an opinion essay about one of the rules in your classroom.

3 On a separate sheet of paper, use your prewriting plan to write an opinion essay, or write an opinion essay on what makes a person a good role model.

Corrective Feedback

IF . . . students have trouble distinguishing between statements of fact and statements of opinion,

THEN . . . have students ask themselves whether the statement can be proved. Explain that even statements that express widely held beliefs are not facts unless they can be proved. For example, *Summer vacation is the best time of the year* might seem like a fact because most students agree with it, but it cannot be proved. Have students practice rewriting popular opinions as facts, such as *Most students in our class do not attend summer school.*

Focus Trait: Voice

Remind students that an author chooses words and phrases that reveal his or her attitude toward a topic. Explain that this is called *voice.*

Students who are late to class can be distracting.

Explain that this sentence states an opinion but doesn't give much detail about how the author feels.

When one student is late to class, the entire class suffers from the distraction.

Point out that words like *one* and *entire*, as well as *suffers*, make it clear that the writer strongly disapproves of students who are late because one person is doing harm to several others. It also lets readers know *why* the writer feels that way.

Explain to students that the words they use to express their opinions should leave the reader with a lasting impression.

Problem-Solution Composition

Minilesson 23

Supporting Solutions with Reasons and Examples

Common Core State Standard: W.5.1

Objective: Support a goal with reasons.

Guiding Question: What reasons best support my position?

Teach/Model—I Do

With students, read and then discuss handbook p. 36. Explain that the model gives several reasons why a student-teacher committee is a good idea. Write *It won't take much time.* Point out that this reason is vague; it would be a stronger reason if it were more specific. Write *The committee would only have to meet for one hour each month.* Explain that this sentence is a better reason because it shows how much time the committee needs.

Guided Practice—We Do

Tell students to imagine they are writing a problem-solution paragraph about litter in the park. Work with them to identify a way to keep the park clean. Help them suggest reasons why the solution is a good one. Write the reasons on the board.

Practice/Apply—You Do

COLLABORATIVE Write a number of problems on the board, such as *no extra help with math*, *no place to play basketball*, and *boring morning announcements*. Have small groups choose one problem and write a solution and reasons and examples that support it.

INDEPENDENT Have students choose another problem from the list and write a solution and reasons and examples that support it.

Conference/Evaluate

If students are having trouble writing reasons that support their position, encourage them to talk with a partner before they write. They can ask their partner if the reasons are convincing.

Minilesson 24

Drafting a Problem-Solution Composition

Common Core State Standard: W.5.1

Objective: Write a problem-solution composition with good supporting reasons.

Guiding Question: How can I present a convincing solution?

Teach/Model—I Do

Review the definition and Parts of a Problem-Solution Composition. Read aloud the model, discussing the solution statement and the boldfaced transitions. Go over the list in the Other Transitions box.

Guided Practice—We Do

 Direct students to the frame on handbook p. 37. Guide them to identify and list reasons to support the solution (examples: *it's more fun for students to volunteer in groups than alone; big team projects would be more exciting than small individual projects*). Help students suggest a conclusion that restates the opinion. Use students' reasons and conclusion to complete the frame. Have students write in their books as you write on the board.

Practice/Apply—You Do

 COLLABORATIVE Have small groups complete Activity 2 with their group's idea of how to decrease lateness. Have them share their work.

 INDEPENDENT Have students read the directions. Tell them to use their prewriting plan from Lesson 12 or to brainstorm a new plan using Graphic Organizer 7.

Conference/Evaluate

As students draft, circulate and help them focus on only reasons that support their position. Evaluate using the rubric on p. 104.

- Problem-Solution Essay
- Adding Details
- Transitions

Problem-Solution Composition

A **problem-solution composition** identifies a problem or situation that should be changed or fixed. Then it suggests a way to solve the problem.

Parts of a Problem-Solution Composition

- A topic sentence that clearly states the problem
- Additional sentences that explain the problem and tell how the writer thinks the problem can be solved
- Sentences offering evidence that the writer's solution is the best one and that it will work
- A concluding sentence that restates and reinforces the writer's position

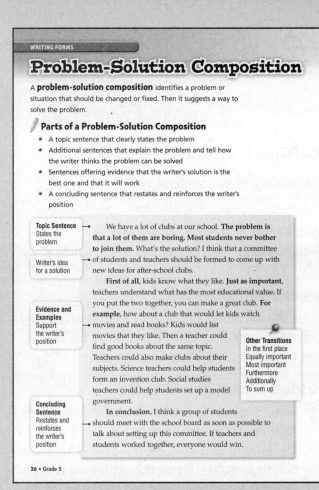

Topic Sentence
States the problem

Writer's idea for a solution

Evidence and Examples
Support the writer's position

Concluding Sentence
Restates and reinforces the writer's position

We have a lot of clubs at our school. **The problem is that a lot of them are boring. Most students never bother to join them.** What's the solution? I think that a committee of students and teachers should be formed to come up with new ideas for after-school clubs.

First of all, kids know what they like. **Just as important**, teachers understand what has the most educational value. If you put the two together, you can make a great club. **For example**, how about a club that would let kids watch movies and read books? Kids would list movies that they like. Then a teacher could find good books about the same topic. Teachers could also make clubs about their subjects. Science teachers could help students form an invention club. Social studies teachers could help students set up a model government.

In conclusion, I think a group of students should meet with the school board as soon as possible to talk about setting up this committee. If teachers and students worked together, everyone would win.

Other Transitions
In the first place
Equally important
Most important
Furthermore
Additionally
To sum up

Name _____

Follow your teacher's directions to complete this page.

1 Many things could be improved in our community with help from volunteers. The problem is that students who could volunteer don't. To fix this, we should arrange special Saturdays when students can volunteer. First of all,

_____
_____
_____. For example, _____
_____
_____
_____
_____
_____. Just as important, _____
_____
_____
_____
_____
In conclusion, _____
_____
_____
_____

2 On a separate sheet of paper, plan and write a problem-solution composition about decreasing lateness among students.

3 On a separate sheet of paper, use your prewriting plan to write a problem-solution composition, or plan and write a composition about a rule you think is a problem such as *no inline skates in stores.*

Corrective Feedback

IF . . . students have trouble identifying a solution to a problem,

THEN . . . have them search online for ideas. For example, to explore possible solutions to the problem of tardiness, students might use a search engine to seek out keywords, such as *discourage tardiness in elementary school.* Students can then browse the results and choose a promising solution to propose in their own paper.

Focus Trait: Organization

Explain that students can strengthen a problem-solution paragraph by ending it with a strong conclusion that restates and reinforces the author's position. Write this example on the board:

In conclusion, it might help to add more tables in the cafeteria so everyone can sit to eat lunch.

Elicit from students how the conclusion can be revised to make it stronger. For example:

Let's add more tables in the cafeteria so that the entire fifth grade can eat together.

In conclusion, we deserve to sit together when we have lunch.

Persuasive Letter

Minilesson 25

Using Business Letter Format

Common Core State Standard: W.5.1

Objective: Write a persuasive letter using business letter format.

Guiding Question: What is business letter format?

Teach/Model—I Do

With students, read and discuss handbook p. 38. Explain that a business letter is more formal than a personal letter because the writer wants to communicate his or her ideas in a serious way, often to someone he or she does not know. Point out the parts of a business letter and their placement: heading, inside address, salutation, body, closing, and signature. Explain that the heading tells the author's address. The inside address tells the recipient's address. In business letter format, the salutation ends with a colon.

Guided Practice—We Do

Tell students to suppose they want to write a persuasive letter to the mayor. Guide them to create the heading, inside address, salutation, closing, and signature for it. Write their suggestions on the board, helping them format each part correctly.

Practice/Apply—You Do

COLLABORATIVE On the board list people to whom students could write a persuasive letter, such as *newspaper editor*, *governor*, or *school committee member*. Have small groups write the heading, inside address, salutation, closing, and signature for a letter addressed to one of these people.

INDEPENDENT Have students use business letter format to write the heading, inside address, salutation, closing, and signature for a persuasive letter addressed to another person on the list.

Conference/Evaluate

Encourage students having trouble writing a correctly formatted letter to line up their text along the left margin, which is also an acceptable format.

Minilesson 26

Drafting a Persuasive Letter

Common Core State Standard: W.5.1

Objective: Write a convincing persuasive letter.

Guiding Question: What are the best reasons to support my goal?

Teach/Model—I Do

Review the definition and Parts of a Persuasive Letter. Read and discuss the model, the opinion, the bold-faced transitions, and Other Closings box.

Guided Practice—We Do

 Direct students to the frame on handbook p. 39. Together, decide on a person you could write the letter to, and fill in the line after *Dear*. Point out the opinion statement and transition. Guide students to suggest ideas and examples for the body before they write, such as *We can get local businesses to donate items for an auction.* Remind students that a real letter would also have a heading, inside address, closing, and signature. Together, choose the best suggestions and write the letter. Have students write in their books as you write on the board.

Practice/Apply—You Do

 COLLABORATIVE Have groups follow directions to plan and complete Activity 2. Have groups share their work.

 INDEPENDENT Have students complete Activity 3. Tell them to use their prewriting plan from Lesson 13 or to brainstorm a new plan using Graphic Organizer 7.

Conference/Evaluate

Circulate and help students choose strong reasons. Evaluate using the rubric on p. 104.

 Digital
- Persuasive Letter
- Persuasive Language
- Transitions

Persuasive Letter

A **persuasive letter** is a type of formal letter. In it, the writer tries to convince the reader to think or act in a certain way.

Parts of a Persuasive Letter

- Business letter format, which includes a heading, inside address, salutation, body, closing, and signature
- A lead sentence that clearly states the writer's goal, or purpose, for writing the letter
- Supporting sentences that give and explain reasons for agreeing with the writer's goal
- A conclusion that restates the writer's goal

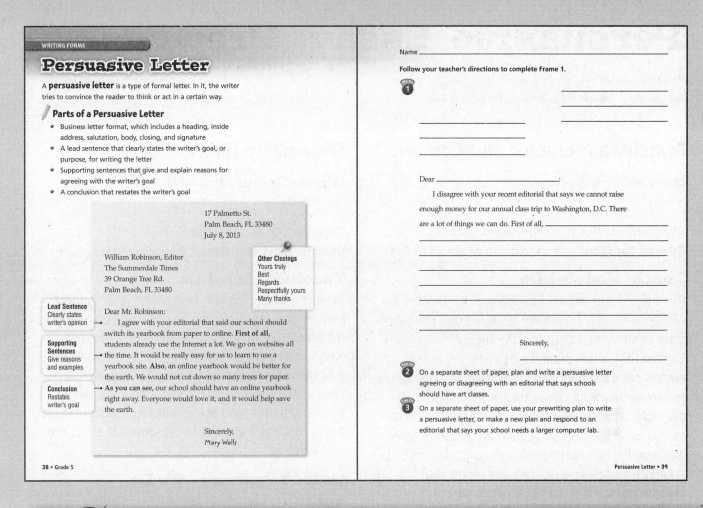

17 Palmetto St.
Palm Beach, FL 33480
July 8, 2013

William Robinson, Editor
The Summerdale Times
39 Orange Tree Rd.
Palm Beach, FL 33480

Other Closings
Yours truly
Best
Regards
Respectfully yours
Many thanks

Lead Sentence
Clearly states writer's opinion

Supporting Sentences
Give reasons and examples

Conclusion
Restates writer's goal

Dear Mr. Robinson:
    I agree with your editorial that said our school should switch its yearbook from paper to online. **First of all**, students already use the Internet a lot. We go on websites all the time. It would be really easy for us to learn to use a yearbook site. **Also**, an online yearbook would be better for the earth. We would not cut down so many trees for paper. **As you can see**, our school should have an online yearbook right away. Everyone would love it, and it would help save the earth.

           Sincerely,
           Mary Wells

Name _____

Follow your teacher's directions to complete Frame 1.

Dear _____ :
    I disagree with your recent editorial that says we cannot raise enough money for our annual class trip to Washington, D.C. There are a lot of things we can do. First of all, _____

Sincerely,
_____

On a separate sheet of paper, plan and write a persuasive letter agreeing or disagreeing with an editorial that says schools should have art classes.

On a separate sheet of paper, use your prewriting plan to write a persuasive letter, or make a new plan and respond to an editorial that says your school needs a larger computer lab.

Corrective Feedback

IF . . . students have trouble making their reasons sound convincing,

THEN . . . show them clippings of newspaper editorials. Have students circle words or phrases that they find especially convincing. Encourage students to emulate this kind of language in their own letters where appropriate.

Focus Trait: Ideas

Explain to students that they can strengthen their persuasive letters by including examples for their reasons. Good examples do not just state what the writer thinks or believes. They give real-life information that shows why the writer's ideas are important.

Together, brainstorm examples to support the reasons given in the student model (examples: *Students use sites like Friendbook to talk to their friends; Millions of trees are cut down every year*).

As students write their own persuasive letters, encourage them to include examples that support their reasons.

Persuasive Essay: Prewriting

Matching Audience and Content

Common Core State Standard: W.5.5

Objective: Match arguments to specific readers.

Guiding Question: How do I convince my specific readers?

Teach/Model—I Do

Read aloud and discuss handbook p. 40. Discuss the components of a persuasive essay, emphasizing the clear opinion statement and the supporting reasons. Explain that, when planning a persuasive essay, writers need to understand that some reasons will be more effective with one audience than another. For example, *a school newspaper will be fun* is a reason that appeals more to students than to school administrators. Explain that writers should think about their audience and choose reasons and words that are likely to persuade those particular readers.

Guided Practice—We Do

On the board, write an opinion statement, such as *we should take an overnight field trip to the state capitol.* With students, generate a list of potential audiences, from young students to parents to school administrators. For each audience elicit two or three concerns this audience might have about the trip, such as safety, cost, fun, or educational content. Write those concerns on the board.

Practice/Apply—You Do

COLLABORATIVE Have each small group choose one potential audience and write three reasons in favor of an overnight field trip. Remind students to make sure their reasons match the concerns you have written down for their chosen audience.

INDEPENDENT Have students choose another audience for the field trip and write three reasons aimed at that particular audience.

Conference/Evaluate

Have students evaluate their reasons to make sure they are tailored to the appropriate audience.

Organizing Ideas

Common Core State Standard: W.5.5

Objective: Organize a persuasive essay.

Guiding Question: What is the best form for my essay?

Teach/Model—I Do

Review handbook p. 41. Discuss the idea-support map, explaining that each box contains one supporting reason for the opinion statement. Note that writers often finish with their strongest reason but that the reasons should flow logically as well. Demonstrate this by pointing out how the model begins with a reason about individual students and then broadens the scope to reasons that affect the whole school.

Guided Practice—We Do

 Direct students to Activity 1 on handbook p. 41. Elicit an opinion statement about tutoring or starting a student help center and write it in the first box. Remind students that this essay will be aimed at other fifth grade students. Guide students to suggest several possible reasons aimed at that particular audience. List their reasons on the board and help students select the three strongest. Together, choose the best order for these reasons and put them in the idea-support map. Have students write in their books as you write on the board.

Practice/Apply—You Do

 COLLABORATIVE Have groups plan and complete Activity 2. Make sure each group selects a target audience.

 INDEPENDENT Have students read and follow the directions. Tell them to use their prewriting plan from Lesson 14 or to brainstorm a new plan using Graphic Organizer 7.

Conference/Evaluate

As students draft, have them evaluate their work using the rubric or on p. 104.

Persuasive Essay: Prewriting

In a **persuasive essay** the writer tries to convince the reader to act or agree with a position. Persuasive writing needs reasons to make it convincing. One way to organize your reasons is to use an idea-support map.

Parts of Prewriting for a Persuasive Essay

- Think of a clear opinion statement
- Write down the reasons to support the opinion, with the most important reason last
- Start thinking of facts and examples to support the reasons you come up with while prewriting

Title or Topic: <u>Starting a School Paper</u>

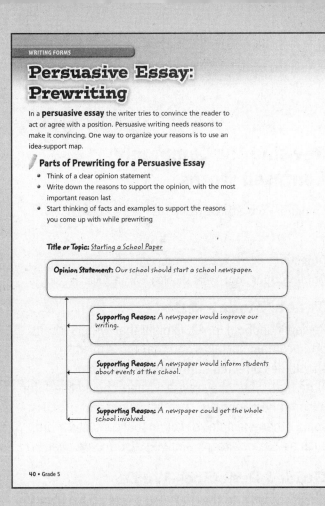

Opinion Statement: Our school should start a school newspaper.

Supporting Reason: A newspaper would improve our writing.

Supporting Reason: A newspaper would inform students about events at the school.

Supporting Reason: A newspaper could get the whole school involved.

Name _____

Follow your teacher's directions to complete this page.

 1 **Title or Topic:** _____

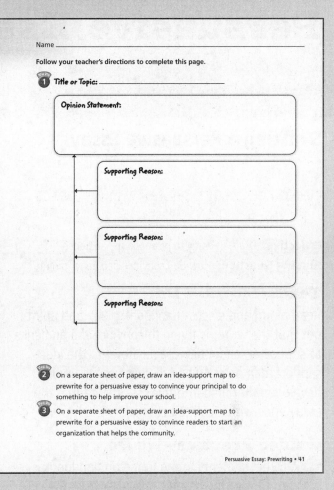

Opinion Statement:

Supporting Reason:

Supporting Reason:

Supporting Reason:

2 On a separate sheet of paper, draw an idea-support map to prewrite for a persuasive essay to convince your principal to do something to help improve your school.

3 On a separate sheet of paper, draw an idea-support map to prewrite for a persuasive essay to convince readers to start an organization that helps the community.

Corrective Feedback

IF . . . students are having a hard time coming up with audience-specific reasons for their opinion,

THEN . . . have them imagine that they are speaking directly to their chosen audience. What things would they say to convince their parents? their friends? their teachers? Tell them to think of issues that might concern each group as well as what words communicate best to that audience.

Focus Trait: Organization

Remind students that, in any essay that has a topic statement and several supporting reasons or details, it is important to put those details in a logical order. Point out that there usually are several possible ways to organize, depending on the topic, the audience, or the supporting reasons. Discuss these options:

- Strongest reason first or last
- Most similar reasons next to each other
- General reasons followed by more specific ones or *vice versa*
- Chronological order
- Most obvious to most unusual, *vice versa*

Emphasize that any organization for the supporting reasons is good, as long as it is chosen for a purpose and the writer uses it for the whole essay.

Persuasive Essay

Minilesson 29

Drafting a Persuasive Essay

Common Core State Standards: W.5.1, W.5.4, W.5.10

Objective: Draft an essay to persuade my audience

Guiding Question: How do I convince people to join me?

Teach/Model—I Do

Read aloud and discuss handbook p. 42, and point out that the writer is trying to convince the audience to support a school newspaper. Refer to the idea-support map on p. 40 and discuss how the writer developed that map into this essay. Note that the essay ends with a call to action.

Guided Practice—We Do

 Direct students to the frame on handbook p. 43. Use the graphic organizer from the previous lesson to work together to write reasons as sentences, such as *First of all, older students can help younger students with their work because they've already studied the subject.* Have students write in their books as you write on the board.

Practice/Apply—You Do

 COLLABORATIVE Have groups complete Activity 2. Tell students they can use their plans from the previous lesson. Remind them to focus on their audience and order their arguments logically.

 INDEPENDENT Have students read and follow the directions. Tell them to use their prewriting plan from the previous lesson.

Conference/Evaluate

As students draft, have them evaluate their work using the rubric on p. 104.

Minilesson 30

Revising for Commonly Confused Words

Common Core State Standards: W.5.1, W.5.4, W.5.5, W.5.10

Objective: Edit to find incorrect word use.

Guiding Question: What should I look for when revising?

Teach/Model—I Do

Review handbook p. 42. Explain that writers' drafts often contain mistakes and that these mistakes should be corrected during the revision process. Note that, when they revise, writers should check for misused homophones, such as *weight* and *wait*. List some other examples of commonly confused words, such as *accept/except, allowed/aloud, bare/bear*.

Guided Practice—We Do

Direct students to the draft you wrote on handbook p. 43. Reread the draft, checking for commonly confused words, such as homophones, and work with students to correct any mistakes. Guide students to check that details are organized logically; move around sentences as necessary.

Practice/Apply—You Do

COLLABORATIVE Have groups reread the drafts they wrote for Minilesson 29 and revise them to fix any confused or misused words. Also have groups check that their drafts are organized logically and make any changes they think are necessary. Have groups check each others' work.

INDEPENDENT Have students reread their drafts from Minilesson 29 or another draft, revising for commonly confused words.

Conference/Evaluate

Circulate and help students revise.

Digital
- eBook
- WriteSmart
- Interactive Lessons

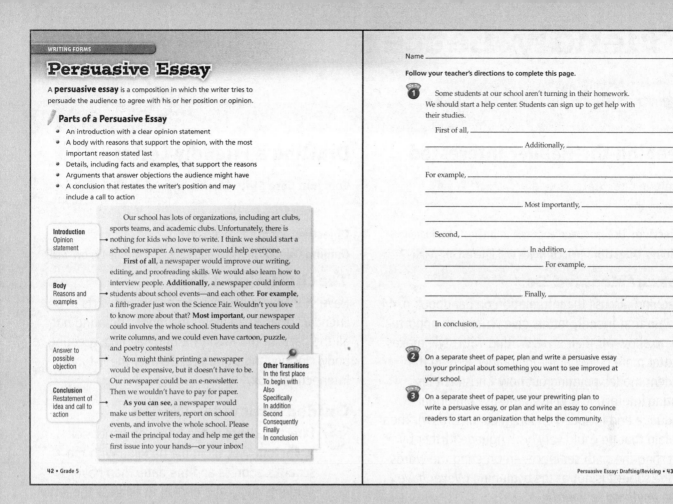

Persuasive Essay

A **persuasive essay** is a composition in which the writer tries to persuade the audience to agree with his or her position or opinion.

Parts of a Persuasive Essay

- An introduction with a clear opinion statement
- A body with reasons that support the opinion, with the most important reason stated last
- Details, including facts and examples, that support the reasons
- Arguments that answer objections the audience might have
- A conclusion that restates the writer's position and may include a call to action

Introduction
Opinion statement

> Our school has lots of organizations, including art clubs, sports teams, and academic clubs. Unfortunately, there is nothing for kids who love to write. I think we should start a school newspaper. A newspaper would help everyone.

Body
Reasons and examples

> **First of all**, a newspaper would improve our writing, editing, and proofreading skills. We would also learn how to interview people. **Additionally**, a newspaper could inform students about school events—and each other. **For example**, a fifth-grader just won the Science Fair. Wouldn't you love to know more about that? **Most important**, our newspaper could involve the whole school. Students and teachers could write columns, and we could even have cartoon, puzzle, and poetry contests!

Answer to possible objection

> You might think printing a newspaper would be expensive, but it doesn't have to be. Our newspaper could be an e-newsletter. Then we wouldn't have to pay for paper.

Conclusion
Restatement of idea and call to action

> **As you can see**, a newspaper would make us better writers, report on school events, and involve the whole school. Please e-mail the principal today and help me get the first issue into your hands—or your inbox!

Other Transitions
In the first place
To begin with
Also
Specifically
In addition
Second
Consequently
Finally
In conclusion

Name _____

Follow your teacher's directions to complete this page.

1 Some students at our school aren't turning in their homework. We should start a help center. Students can sign up to get help with their studies.

First of all, _____

_____ Additionally, _____

_____

For example, _____

_____

_____ Most importantly, _____

_____

Second, _____

_____ In addition, _____

_____ For example, _____

_____

_____ Finally, _____

In conclusion, _____

_____

2 On a separate sheet of paper, plan and write a persuasive essay to your principal about something you want to see improved at your school.

3 On a separate sheet of paper, use your prewriting plan to write a persuasive essay, or plan and write an essay to convince readers to start an organization that helps the community.

Corrective Feedback

IF . . . students are having a hard time writing a conclusion,

THEN . . . have them summarize their argument out loud and explain why it is important. This summary can be a good starting place for their conclusion.

Focus Trait: Word Choice

Revision is an important step in the essay-writing process. In addition to unnecessary ideas, word choice errors should be eliminated in the revision stage.

When revising an essay, writers should also look out for these errors:

Wordiness: using more words than is necessary, such as "due to the fact that" instead of "because"

Misused Words: vocabulary words that don't mean what you think they mean (using *sanitary* instead of *safe*)

Jargon: words specific to a certain body of knowledge, like science or sports terms

Slang: words and phrases used in casual speech but not in academic writing ("The British Parliament was *freaked out* that American colonists were *disrespecting* the king.")

Grade 5 • 43

Friendly Letter

Minilesson 31

Keeping the Reader Interested

Common Core State Standards: W.5.3b, W.5.4

Objective: Use language and style to interest the audience.
Guiding Question: Which words will interest my reader?

Teach/Model—I Do

Read and discuss the information on handbook p. 44. Explain that friendly letters give writers an opportunity to show off their style. Writing with style makes a letter more personal for the reader. Reread the student model, pointing out how Chris kept his writing interesting and lively. He used informal language and included an interjection (*Gross!*). Then explain that he could vary his language further by inverting the sixth sentence—reordering the words so the subject is not at the beginning (*Never have I seen anything so weird!*).

Guided Practice—We Do

On the board, write *There was a noise. It was a crash. It was a bit frightening. A squirrel crawled out of the bush. We felt better.* Explain to students that you want to make these sentences more interesting for readers. Together, add interjections, invert word order (in the fourth sentence), and use informal language to improve the sentences.

Practice/Apply—You Do

COLLABORATIVE On the board, write *The hike was after the cookout. The hike was rather fun. We saw the sunset. It was beautiful.* Have students improve the sentences by inverting word order in the first sentence, adding interjections, and making the language informal.

INDEPENDENT Have students improve the following: *My cousin Amelia is not only funny but also adventurous. She is fond of spicy food. I tried her favorite kind of pepper. It made my eyes water.*

Conference/Evaluate

Have students identify and use inverted sentences in books as models for their own writing.

Minilesson 32

Drafting a Friendly Letter

Common Core State Standards: W.5.3b, W.5.3c, W.5.4

Objective: Write a friendly letter.
Guiding Question: What do I write to someone I know well?

Teach/Model—I Do

Have students review the definition and Parts of a Friendly Letter. Read aloud the model, pointing out all the parts of the friendly letter: heading, greeting, body, closing, and signature. Go over the list in the Interjections box.

Guided Practice—We Do

 Direct students to the frame on handbook p. 45. Together, fill in the heading with the school's address and the date. Then have students suggest a person to address the letter to, and write the name on the line after *Dear*. Elicit from students an exciting or cool sight they would describe in a letter (such as *baby seal riding on its mother's back*), and use their suggestions to complete the second sentence of the frame. Use students' suggestions to continue the letter with details that will interest their audience. As you write, remind students to keep their language interesting and informal. Have students write in their books as you write on the board.

Practice/Apply—You Do

 COLLABORATIVE Have small groups complete Activity 2. Encourage them to include inverted sentences and interjections.

 INDEPENDENT Have students read the directions. Tell them to use their plan from Lesson 16 or to brainstorm a new plan using Graphic Organizer 7.

Conference/Evaluate

As students draft, circulate and help them choose details that will interest their reader. Evaluate using the rubric on p. 104.

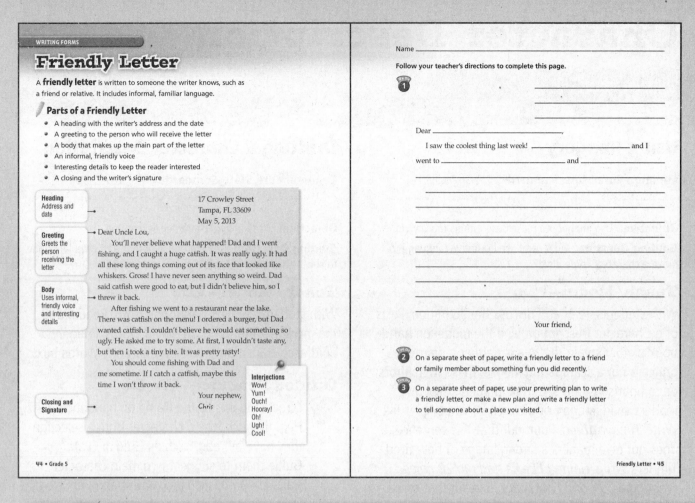

Friendly Letter

A **friendly letter** is written to someone the writer knows, such as a friend or relative. It includes informal, familiar language.

Parts of a Friendly Letter

- A heading with the writer's address and the date
- A greeting to the person who will receive the letter
- A body that makes up the main part of the letter
- An informal, friendly voice
- Interesting details to keep the reader interested
- A closing and the writer's signature

Heading
Address and date

Greeting
Greets the person receiving the letter

Body
Uses informal, friendly voice and interesting details

Closing and Signature

17 Crowley Street
Tampa, FL 33609
May 5, 2013

Dear Uncle Lou,

You'll never believe what happened! Dad and I went fishing, and I caught a huge catfish. It was really ugly. It had all these long things coming out of its face that looked like whiskers. Gross! I have never seen anything so weird. Dad said catfish were good to eat, but I didn't believe him, so I threw it back.

After fishing we went to a restaurant near the lake. There was catfish on the menu! I ordered a burger, but Dad wanted catfish. I couldn't believe he would eat something so ugly. He asked me to try some. At first, I wouldn't taste any, but then I took a tiny bite. It was pretty tasty!

You should come fishing with Dad and me sometime. If I catch a catfish, maybe this time I won't throw it back.

Your nephew,
Chris

Interjections
Wow!
Yum!
Ouch!
Hooray!
Oh!
Ugh!
Cool!

Name _____

Follow your teacher's directions to complete this page.

Dear _____,

I saw the coolest thing last week! _____ and I went to _____ and _____

Your friend,
_____

  On a separate sheet of paper, write a friendly letter to a friend or family member about something fun you did recently.

3 On a separate sheet of paper, use your prewriting plan to write a friendly letter, or make a new plan and write a friendly letter to tell someone about a place you visited.

✔ Corrective Feedback

IF . . . students are having trouble choosing an audience for their letter,

THEN . . . have them ask themselves *Whom do I know who shares my interests? Who would be most interested in reading about this place I like to visit?* Encourage students to think if they have ever been someplace similar to the place they are writing about. If so, they may want to write to someone who was on the original trip.

Focus Trait: Voice

Tell students that writing with style is the same thing as writing with voice. The words and sentence structures a writer uses may keep the reader interested, but they also show what the writer is like. Explain that two people witnessing the same event would react differently and describe it in different ways. Compare:

I trembled as I climbed up the ladder. Jumping off the high diving board was the most terrifying thing I have ever done!

with:

I scrambled up the ladder as fast as I could. I had been imagining leaping from the high diving board for weeks!

As students write their friendly letters, encourage them to describe their feelings and reactions in ways that show what their personalities are like.

Character Description

Minilesson 33

Using Imagery

Common Core State Standards: W.5.3b, W.5.3d

Objective: Use imagery to make descriptions more vivid.

Guiding Question: How can I use figurative language to make a character come alive?

Teach/Model—I Do

With students, read and discuss the definition, Parts of a Character Description, and the model on handbook p. 46. Explain that Aja is neither a warrior princess nor a scampering mouse. These metaphors, or comparisons, are a kind of imagery: they give readers vivid images, or pictures, of what Aja is like. Write *Tim was tired.* Point out that this sentence does not give readers a strong image of how tired Tim felt. Write *Tim felt like he had run 20 miles wearing a 50-pound backpack.* Explain that these details give readers a mental image that helps convey just how tired Tim felt.

Guided Practice—We Do

Tell students to think about a boy or a girl walking outside on a cold day. Work together to make a list of images showing how cold the character is, what he or she looks like, and how he or she feels.

Practice/Apply—You Do

COLLABORATIVE Write several topics on the board, such as *visiting relatives, reading a report to the class,* and *eating a favorite food.* Have small groups choose a topic and write a list of images they might use in a description of the activity.

INDEPENDENT Have students choose another topic from the list on the board; have them repeat the activity above.

Conference/Evaluate

Encourage any student having trouble using imagery to try thinking of something else that is like what he or she is trying to describe.

Minilesson 34

Drafting a Character Description

Common Core State Standards: W.5.3b, W.5.3d

Objective: Write a vivid character description.

Guiding Question: How can I use details and vivid language to show how a character looks, acts, and feels?

Teach/Model—I Do

With students, review handbook p. 46. Read aloud the model, pointing out the vivid words, imagery, boldfaced transitions, and the Character Words box.

Guided Practice—We Do

 Direct students to the frame on handbook p. 47. Help them choose a character from a selection they have all read, such as Greg in "Laff." Guide them to suggest two main character traits for Greg, such as *creative* and *persistent.* Help students find examples from "Laff" (*creative: writes his own comic books; draws all the pictures; persistent: works hard on his drawings; keeps trying till he prints his comics correctly*). List the ideas on the board. Then have students suggest sentences to complete the frame. Have students write in their books as you write on the board.

Practice/Apply—You Do

 COLLABORATIVE Have small groups plan and complete the activity. Discuss their work.

 INDEPENDENT Have students read the directions and use their prewriting plan from Lesson 17 or brainstorm a new plan using Graphic Organizer 1 or 15.

Conference/Evaluate

Circulate and help students choose details and imagery that will bring their descriptions to life. Evaluate using the rubric on p. 104.

Digital
• Fictional Narrative;
• Character Description;
• Transitions

Character Description

A **character description** shows how someone looks, acts, and feels. It tells about the person's character, or personality.

Parts of a Character Description

- Main ideas that tell about the person's character
- Examples of the person's words and actions
- Vivid details about the person's appearance and actions
- Dialogue that shows how the person talks and what the person thinks and feels

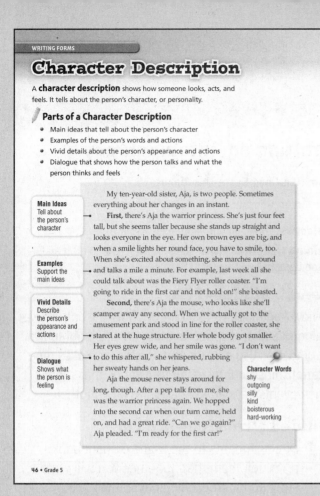

Main Ideas
Tell about the person's character

Examples
Support the main ideas

Vivid Details
Describe the person's appearance and actions

Dialogue
Shows what the person is feeling

My ten-year-old sister, Aja, is two people. Sometimes everything about her changes in an instant.

First, there's Aja the warrior princess. She's just four feet tall, but she seems taller because she stands up straight and looks everyone in the eye. Her own brown eyes are big, and when a smile lights her round face, you have to smile, too. When she's excited about something, she marches around and talks a mile a minute. For example, last week all she could talk about was the Fiery Flyer roller coaster. "I'm going to ride in the first car and not hold on!" she boasted.

Second, there's Aja the mouse, who looks like she'll scamper away any second. When we actually got to the amusement park and stood in line for the roller coaster, she stared at the huge structure. Her whole body got smaller. Her eyes grew wide, and her smile was gone. "I don't want to do this after all," she whispered, rubbing her sweaty hands on her jeans.

Aja the mouse never stays around for long, though. After a pep talk from me, she was the warrior princess again. We hopped into the second car when our turn came, held on, and had a great ride. "Can we go again?" Aja pleaded. "I'm ready for the first car!"

Character Words
shy
outgoing
silly
kind
boisterous
hard-working

Name _____

Follow your teacher's directions to complete this page.

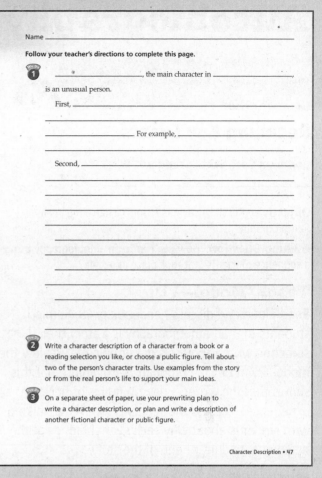

1 _____, the main character in _____, is an unusual person.

First, _____

_____ For example, _____

Second, _____

_____

_____

_____

_____

_____

_____

_____

_____

_____

2 Write a character description of a character from a book or a reading selection you like, or choose a public figure. Tell about two of the person's character traits. Use examples from the story or from the real person's life to support your main ideas.

3 On a separate sheet of paper, use your prewriting plan to write a character description, or plan and write a description of another fictional character or public figure.

 ## Corrective Feedback

IF . . . students are unable to describe what someone looks like,

THEN . . . have them brainstorm words and images, using a web. They can write the name of what they want to describe in the center oval (example: *hair*). Then they can write words that describe the feature in the other four ovals. Tell them to include a comparison in at least one oval (examples: *long, black as coal, tied with a red ribbon, shiny*).

 ## Focus Trait: Word Choice

Remind students that adjectives are words that describe people, places, and things. A good description has plenty of adjectives to help the reader picture what the writer is describing. Adjectives may tell *what kind, how many,* or *which one.*

Write a few simple sentences on the board, such as

Steven rode a train through the mountains.
The student studied for hours.
Sharon's dress caught in the wind.

Work with students to make these sentences more descriptive:

Steven rode a speedy train through the huge mountains.
The math student studied for two hours.
Sharon's red dress caught in the blustery wind.

Autobiography

Recalling Key Events

Common Core State Standard: W.5.8

Objective: Recall key events to form a narrative in an autobiography.

Guiding Question: How can I write an autobiography using a sequence of events that took place in my life?

Teach/Model—I Do

Read aloud and discuss handbook p. 48. Remind students that an autobiography is a story that someone writes about his or her own life. Review the model. Point out the pronoun *I*, explaining that this shows that the writer is describing his or her own experiences. Discuss the sequence of events, talking with students about why each event belongs at the beginning, middle, or end of the story.

Guided Practice—We Do

With the class, discuss a memorable occasion you enjoyed together, such as a special gathering at the school or a field trip. Have students brainstorm a chronological list of the events that took place. Work with students to place the events at the appropriate points at the story's beginning, middle, and end.

Practice/Apply—You Do

COLLABORATIVE On the board, write *A Good Time Was Had by All.* Have groups get together and discuss a day that they all enjoyed together. Have students write down a sequence of events for that day, placing them at the beginning, middle, or end of the story.

INDEPENDENT Tell students to choose a day when something unusual happened at school. Have them list the key events of that day, placing the events at the beginning, middle, and end of the story.

Conference/Evaluate

Have students check to make sure events are properly placed at the beginning, middle, and end. As needed, discuss with them why certain events belong at the beginning or at the end.

Drafting an Autobiography

Common Core State Standards: W.5.3, W.5.8

Objective: Draft an autobiography.

Guiding Question: What steps should I take to draft an autobiography?

Teach/Model—I Do

Review handbook p. 48. Point out how the author uses dialogue and description to bring an autobiographical story to life. Also discuss how the writer makes time relationships clear by using transitions that show when events happen in relation to one another.

Guided Practice—We Do

 Direct students to the frame on handbook p. 49. Tell them that, together, you will write a story about an exciting day in their lives. Remind them to include dialogue and description as well as transitions. Have students write in their books as you write on the board.

Practice/Apply—You Do

 COLLABORATIVE Have groups plan and complete Activity 2. Encourage them to use dialogue and description and to use transitions to make clear the sequence of events. Remind students that the beginning should introduce who and what the story is about, the middle should retell the main events, and the ending should show how things worked out.

 INDEPENDENT Have students read and follow the directions. Remind them that dialogue and description will help bring their stories to life. Tell them to use their prewriting plan from Lesson 18 or to brainstorm a new plan using Graphic Organizer 5.

Conference/Evaluate

As students draft, have them evaluate their work using the rubric on p. 104.

- eBook
- WriteSmart
- Interactive Lessons

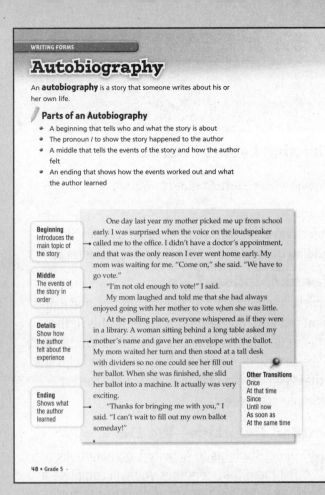

Autobiography

An **autobiography** is a story that someone writes about his or her own life.

Parts of an Autobiography

- A beginning that tells who and what the story is about
- The pronoun *I* to show the story happened to the author
- A middle that tells the events of the story and how the author felt
- An ending that shows how the events worked out and what the author learned

Beginning
Introduces the main topic of the story

Middle
The events of the story in order

Details
Show how the author felt about the experience

Ending
Shows what the author learned

One day last year my mother picked me up from school early. I was surprised when the voice on the loudspeaker called me to the office. I didn't have a doctor's appointment, and that was the only reason I ever went home early. My mom was waiting for me. "Come on," she said. "We have to go vote."

"I'm not old enough to vote!" I said.

My mom laughed and told me that she had always enjoyed going with her mother to vote when she was little.

At the polling place, everyone whispered as if they were in a library. A woman sitting behind a long table asked my mother's name and gave her an envelope with the ballot. My mom waited her turn and then stood at a tall desk with dividers so no one could see her fill out her ballot. When she was finished, she slid her ballot into a machine. It actually was very exciting.

"Thanks for bringing me with you," I said. "I can't wait to fill out my own ballot someday!"

Other Transitions
Once
At that time
Since
Until now
As soon as
At the same time

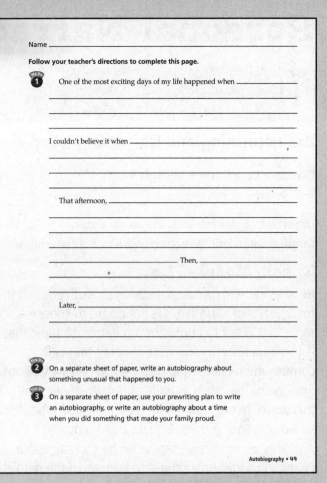

Name _____

Follow your teacher's directions to complete this page.

 1 One of the most exciting days of my life happened when _____
_____
_____

I couldn't believe it when _____
_____
_____

That afternoon, _____
_____

_____ Then, _____

Later, _____
_____

2 On a separate sheet of paper, write an autobiography about something unusual that happened to you.

3 On a separate sheet of paper, use your prewriting plan to write an autobiography, or write an autobiography about a time when you did something that made your family proud.

Corrective Feedback

IF . . . students are having difficulty deciding which events to include in their autobiography,

THEN . . . tell them to think about what their audience will already know about the events of their story. For example, if a story is about the first day of school, the writer can assume that most readers will know certain things about what happens that day. Tell students to focus on unusual events and their own feelings about what happened, not on providing details about places and events that readers might know and understand already.

Focus Trait: Voice

Explain to students that voice is the style or personality that comes through in a piece of writing. In an autobiography, the voice that should come through is that of the writer. Write:

I was surprised to see my little sister standing in front of a crowd of people singing "Twinkle Twinkle Little Star."

Then rewrite the sentence to show students how it can be changed so that it not only reveals more

about the writer but also makes the writing more interesting:

When I saw my shy little sister standing in front of a crowd of people loudly singing "Twinkle Twinkle Little Star," I almost fell to the floor with shock.

Personal Narrative: Prewriting

Minilesson 37

Brainstorming and Narrowing a Topic

Common Core State Standard: W.5.8

Objective: Brainstorm ideas and narrow a topic.
Guiding Question: How do I choose a topic for a narrative?

Teach/Model—I Do

Read aloud and discuss handbook p. 50. Explain that, for a personal narrative, it is important to choose a topic that is not too broad or too narrow. A topic that is too broad could have a lot of detail that will confuse the reader. A topic that is too narrow will not give the writer much to write about. Point out that this writer tells a story about a dog, Peanut, who saved a science project. Explain that there are probably many things that the writer can say about Peanut, but this writer chose to keep all of the details related to this one story.

Guided Practice—We Do

On the board, work with students to brainstorm ideas for personal narratives, such as *unusual foods* or *best presents.* Help students narrow their topics to something appropriate for a personal narrative, such as *the most unusual food I ever tried* or *the best present I ever got.*

Practice/Apply—You Do

COLLABORATIVE Have groups choose a different narrative idea from the list on the board and then narrow it into a good topic for a personal narrative.

INDEPENDENT Have students choose another idea from the list and brainstorm possible topics for a narrative. Have them narrow their topic.

Conference/Evaluate

Have students evaluate their topics and help them determine if each is too narrow or too broad.

Minilesson 38

Planning Events in Order

Common Core State Standard: W.5.5

Objective: Plan events in a personal narrative in order.
Guiding Question: In what order did the events happen?

Teach/Model—I Do

Review handbook p. 50. Read aloud the model and point out how the writer organizes events in the order in which they happened, which helps the story make sense. Point out how the flow chart helps the writer keep the events organized in the correct chronological order.

Guided Practice—We Do

 Direct students to Activity 1 on handbook p. 51. Tell them that, together, you will complete a flow chart for a personal narrative about something scary that happened to them. Work with students to brainstorm an opening sentence. Help students complete the chart with events that relate to the idea. Have students write in their books as you write on the board.

Practice/Apply—You Do

 COLLABORATIVE Have groups plan and complete Activity 2. Remind them to make sure that their events are listed in chronological order. Have groups share what they have written.

 INDEPENDENT Have students read and follow the directions. Tell them to use their prewriting plan from Lesson 19 or to brainstorm a new plan using Graphic Organizer 4.

Conference/Evaluate

As students draft, have them evaluate their work using the rubric on p. 104.

 Digital
- eBook
- WriteSmart
- Interactive Lessons

Personal Narrative: Prewriting

A **personal narrative** tells a story about an important experience in the writer's life and how it made the writer feel.

Parts of Prewriting for a Personal Narrative

- Brainstorm ideas for your personal narrative
- List the important events you will describe in your narrative in a graphic organizer, such as a flow chart
- Make sure the events in your flow chart are in the correct chronological, or time, order

I got my dog Peanut right before I started third grade.	Dad tripped while carrying the model and Mars and Venus rolled out.
He ran around and barked like a crazy little nut, so I named him Peanut.	The planets rolled under a porch where we could not reach them.
Peanut was always with me once I brought him home.	I told Peanut to fetch the balls.
I made a model of the solar system for my final science project.	Peanut got the model planets without breaking them.
My dad, Peanut, and I walked to school with my model.	My model was saved.

Name _____

Follow your teacher's directions to complete this page.

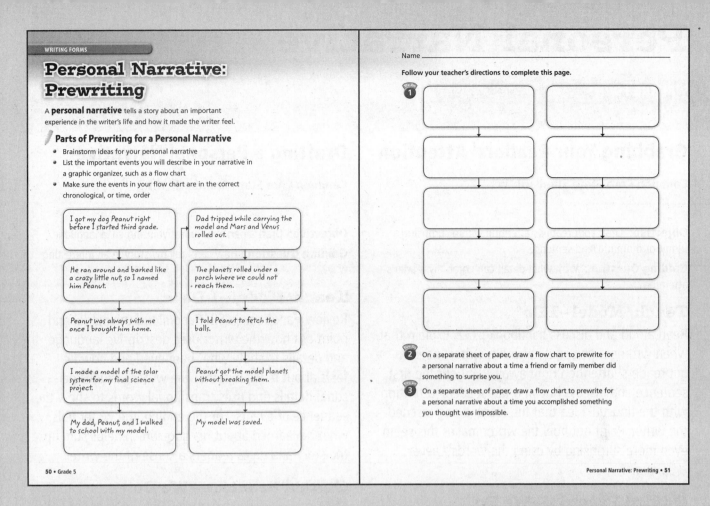

2 On a separate sheet of paper, draw a flow chart to prewrite for a personal narrative about a time a friend or family member did something to surprise you.

3 On a separate sheet of paper, draw a flow chart to prewrite for a personal narrative about a time you accomplished something you thought was impossible.

✓ Corrective Feedback

IF . . . students are having a hard time narrowing their topic,

THEN . . . once they have an idea for a narrative, have them list all the events that happened that are related to it. Tell them to go through the list and cross out events that do not add interest to the narrative. For example, in a narrative about winning a hockey game, *I studied for my math test* may be an event that occurred that same day, but it is not directly related to the story.

Focus Trait: Ideas

Tell students that, when they plan a personal narrative, it is important to make sure that the events in the story relate to their original idea. It helps to ask, "What does this add to my story?" or "How does this event relate to my story idea?" It is also important to write those events in chronological order. Otherwise, the original idea for the narrative gets lost, and the reader becomes confused.

Model the idea-narrowing process on the board. Ask students to give you ideas for a narrative and choose one. Then ask students to listen as you tell the story, having them stop you whenever the story veers away from the original narrative idea. Periodically throw in an event that obviously does not really relate to the story idea. This helps students begin to think about which ideas belong in the narrative and which do not.

Personal Narrative

Minilesson 39

Grabbing Your Readers' Attention

Common Core State Standard: W.5.3d

Objective: Grab your reader's attention with a surprising, funny, or dramatic lead sentence.

Guiding Question: With what detail can I grab my reader's attention?

Teach/Model—I Do

Read aloud and discuss handbook p. 52. Explain that, when writing a personal narrative, writers need to get readers' attention right away. Point out the first sentence and discuss how it grabs readers' attention with the unusual idea that the rescued dog rescued the writer. Point out how the writer makes this seem even more surprising by using the words *I never dreamed.*

Guided Practice—We Do

With students, brainstorm a list of important experiences in students' lives, such as *The most unusual advice I ever got* and write them on the board. Work with students to write a lead sentence for one of the experiences. Emphasize that this lead sentence should grab readers' attention.

Practice/Apply—You Do

COLLABORATIVE Have groups choose another experience from the list. Tell them to list five interesting details or feelings about the experience and use one of those details to write a vivid lead sentence. Have students share their sentences.

INDEPENDENT Have students choose another experience from the list and write an attention-grabbing lead sentence.

Conference/Evaluate

Have students evaluate their lead sentences to make sure they include interesting details and attention-grabbing language.

Minilesson 40

Drafting a Personal Narrative

Common Core State Standard: W.5.5

Objective: Draft a personal narrative using vivid language.

Guiding Question: How can I tell my story in an interesting way?

Teach/Model—I Do

Review handbook p. 52. Read aloud the model and point out how the writer uses descriptive language and details to show what happened and how he feels about it. Explain that the writer includes personal details and uses transitional words to show the sequence of events. For the ending, the writer tells what he learned about his dog, which helps sum up the story and gives readers a sense of the writer.

Guided Practice—We Do

 Direct students to the frame on handbook p. 53. Tell them that, together, you will plan and draft a personal narrative about something scary that happened to them. Help students brainstorm an opening sentence, such as *You'll never guess what happened to me!* Help students complete the frame, putting events in chronological order and using vivid language that keeps readers interested. Have students write in their books as you write on the board.

Practice/Apply—You Do

 COLLABORATIVE Have groups complete Activity 2. Remind them to begin with an attention-grabbing sentence. Have groups share what they have written.

 INDEPENDENT Have students read and follow the directions. Tell them to use their prewriting plan from Lesson 20 or to brainstorm a new plan using Graphic Organizer 4 or 5.

Conference/Evaluate

As students draft, have them evaluate their work using the rubric on p. 104.

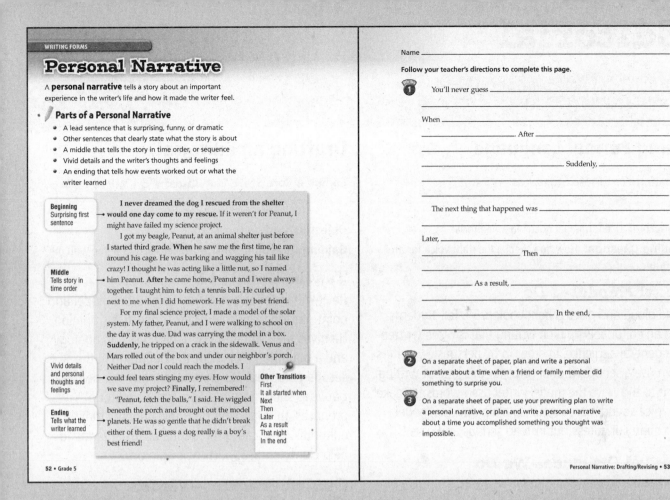

Corrective Feedback

IF . . . students are having a hard time writing an engaging lead sentence,

THEN . . . suggest that they write the story first and add the lead sentence later. First, they can draft the basic plot of their narrative. When they have finished, they can go back to the beginning and use their completed story to help spark a surprising, funny, or dramatic lead sentence.

Focus Trait: Voice

Tell students that, when they are writing a personal narrative, it is important to make sure that they tell the story in their own voice. To do this, they should think of themselves as sitting down and telling the story to a friend. This will help them use vivid language and include personal thoughts and feelings related to the events of the story.

Model the use of voice by writing a three-sentence retelling of a story about something that happened to you. Be sure to write it with no personal emotion, no description, and no humor. Then retell the same story, again in three sentences, but this time including personal emotion, descriptive language, and humor.

Ask students which story is more interesting and which sounds more like it happened to you. Point out that the use of personal voice in a narrative makes it more realistic and also keeps readers interested.

Editorial

Minilesson 41

Using Formal Language

Common Core State Standards: W.5.1a, L.5.6

Objective: Use formal language in an editorial.

Guiding Question: How do I choose the right voice for an editorial?

Teach/Model—I Do

Read aloud and discuss handbook p. 54. Tell students that an editorial is opinion writing that is often written to a general audience. In order to be persuasive, writers often use a serious, formal voice for this kind of writing. Point to the ways the model writer used words to make his voice sound more formal. Explain that the model isn't chatty or cutesy but instead serious and direct.

Guided Practice—We Do

On the board, write an opinion, such as *3D movies are better than 2D movies.* Work with students to come up with a few reasons and write them on the board. Then work together to turn students' suggestions into sentences that use formal language, such as *Movies in 3D are sharper and have better effects.*

Practice/Apply—You Do

COLLABORATIVE Write several other opinions for editorials, such as *video games can make people healthier* or *our town needs an art museum.* Have groups choose a topic, come up with a few reasons to support it, and then write sentences using formal language.

INDEPENDENT Have students choose another opinion and write a few sentences using formal language.

Conference/Evaluate

Circulate and help students choose words and phrases that sound more formal. Remind them to avoid using slang or contractions.

Minilesson 42

Drafting an Editorial

Common Core State Standards: W.5.1, W.5.2b

Objective: Write an editorial.

Guiding Question: What will make readers agree with me?

Teach/Model—I Do

Review handbook p. 54. Read aloud the model and point out the ways the writer supports his opinion. He gives facts and details, and he uses an analogy and a definition. Point out the definition in the second paragraph. Explain that the writer defines *public* to show how the *Sun Times*'s editorial proposes an unfair solution. Tell students that, in editorials, they can often define abstract terms to help clarify and support their opinion.

Guided Practice—We Do

 Direct students to the frame on handbook p. 55 and read the opening. Work with students to write a definition that would support and explain the opinion. (*Example: ...to educate is "to provide with information; inform." The water park would provide us with lots of information. The wave pool could teach us about the tides.*) Together, complete the frame with reasons and an analogy. Have students write in their books as you write on the board.

Practice/Apply—You Do

 COLLABORATIVE Have groups plan and complete Activity 2. Tell them they can use the definition of *volunteer* to tell whether it is fair or unfair to require volunteer work. Have groups share what they have written.

 INDEPENDENT Have students read and follow the directions. Tell them to use the definition of *community* to tell if there are any reasons citizens should help each other.

Conference/Evaluate

As students draft, have them evaluate their work using the rubric on p. 104.

Editorial

An **editorial** is a kind of persuasive essay that appears in a periodical, such as a newspaper, magazine, or website. Some editorials respond to other articles or editorials.

Parts of an Editorial

- An introduction that states the writer's opinion or goal
- Facts and details that support the opinion
- Analogies and definitions that clarify the writer's point
- References to information sources or other texts
- A conclusion that restates the opinion

Introduction
States the writer's opinion and refers to a source

Definition

Facts and Details
Support the writer's opinion

Analogy

Conclusion
Gives a call to action

Keep the Library Open on Weekends

In a recent editorial, the *Sun Times* said, "Budget cuts are needed. Closing the public library on weekends to everyone but university students will save money and do little harm." I strongly disagree. Little money will be saved, and great harm may be done.

By definition, a *public* place is a place for everyone. Denying some people access to the public library is unfair. **In addition,** it does not cost much to keep the library open on weekends. Only four librarians are on duty, and two of them are unpaid volunteers. I also believe that cutting library hours really will harm citizens. **For example,** students without reference materials at home will be unable to work on school reports. **Also,** for busy people like me, the weekend is the only time we can read for pleasure. A weekend without books would be like a Fourth of July without fireworks!

As you can see, closing the library on weekends will do more harm than good. The city should keep it open seven days a week.

Other Transitions
In the first place
To begin with
Additionally
As an example
In conclusion

Reid Daly
Miami, FL 33299

54 • Grade 5

Name _____

Follow your teacher's directions to complete this page.

 1   The members of our school board have said that their biggest concern when choosing a field trip location is to pick one that will "educate and enlighten students." I think Riverside Water Park would be a perfect field trip location.

By definition, to *educate* is _____

_____ In addition, _____

_____

For example, _____

_____

_____ Also, _____

_____

As you can see, _____

_____

_____

 2 On a separate sheet of paper, plan and write an editorial telling whether you think your school should require all students to do volunteer work. Include a definition of a word, such as *volunteer*, to help make your point clear.

3 On a separate sheet of paper, plan and write an editorial to convince readers to start a community food bank. Include a definition of a word, such as *community*.

Editorial • 55

✔ Corrective Feedback

IF . . . students are struggling to restate their opinions in a conclusion,

THEN . . . list some opinions, such as *school should be open all year round* and have them conclude a "pretend" essay with a restatement for or against the opinion.

Focus Trait: Voice

Tell students that writers make their voice more persuasive by sounding interested in or excited about their topic. They are also respectful. Write a few examples of sentences on the board that are informal or disrespectful, such as:

I guess everyone should wash their hands. It's stupid when people don't. It's not like it takes a lot of time. Or, fine, don't wash your hands. You might as well eat off the floor, though.

Ask students to help you revise this paragraph to sound interested in the topic and respectful to readers. For example:

Everyone should wash their hands. It's a smart thing to do. It hardly takes any time at all. Washing your hands will prevent you from catching or spreading germs.

Response to Literature

Minilesson 43

Going Beyond Summarizing

Common Core State Standards: W.5.1a, W.5.1b

Objective: Back up your opinion.

Guiding Question: Which examples back up my opinion?

Teach/Model—I Do

Read aloud and discuss handbook p. 56. Explain that a writer's response to literature expresses his or her opinion about the text. Explain that, instead of giving the reader a simple summary or general list of events in the text, the writer chooses only the events from the text that back up his or her opinion. Point out the writer's opinion in the first paragraph. On the board, write *She wants to clean up the school and make the classrooms nice by putting flowers in them.* Discuss with students the details in this sentence that support the writer's opinion.

Guided Practice—We Do

On the board, write the name of a well-known literary character, such as Harry Potter. Work with students to write an opinion statement about the character, starting with the prompt, *I think Harry is _____ because _____.* Guide them to list four things the character does that support their opinion.

Practice/Apply—You Do

COLLABORATIVE On the board, write several other names of characters from literature, such as Robin Hood, Mowgli, or other characters your students know. Have groups choose one character and write an opinion statement about that character, with a list of four actions to support their opinion.

INDEPENDENT Have students choose a literary character from a story they have recently read and write an opinion statement about that character, with a list of four actions supporting their opinion.

Conference/Evaluate

Have students evaluate their opinion statements and actions to make sure the actions support their opinion.

Minilesson 44

Drafting a Response to Literature

Common Core State Standards: W.5.1a, W.5.4

Objective: Organize details to support your response.

Guiding Question: How can I prove my response is reasonable?

Teach/Model—I Do

Review handbook p. 56. Read aloud the model and point out how the writer supports his or her opinion by comparing details about two of the characters. Point out the last sentence in the second paragraph, which uses details from the story to reach a conclusion. Tell students that one way to organize supporting details in a response is to compare and contrast characters or events.

Guided Practice—We Do

 Direct students to the frame on handbook p. 57. Tell them that together you will write a response to a biography. Work with students to find details from James Forten's life that are different from the lives of children today. Model comparing and contrasting biographical details, using a Venn diagram. Tell students that the contrasting details are the ones that will support the opinion statement. Have students write in their books as you write on the board.

Practice/Apply—You Do

 COLLABORATIVE Have groups plan and complete Activity 2. Tell them they can make a list of Omakayas's characteristics and actions that support their explanation. Have groups share what they have written.

 INDEPENDENT Have students read and follow the directions. Tell them to use their prewriting plan from Lesson 22 or to brainstorm a new plan using Graphic Organizer 7.

Conference/Evaluate

As students draft, have them evaluate their work using the rubric on p. 104.

Response to Literature

A **response to literature** expresses an opinion about the theme, characters, plot, setting, or style of a piece of literature.

Parts of a Response to Literature

- An introduction that expresses an opinion about the text
- A summary about part or all of a story.
- A body that includes reasons that back up the opinion
- Examples from the text to support those reasons
- Details organized logically
- A conclusion that restates the writer's opinion

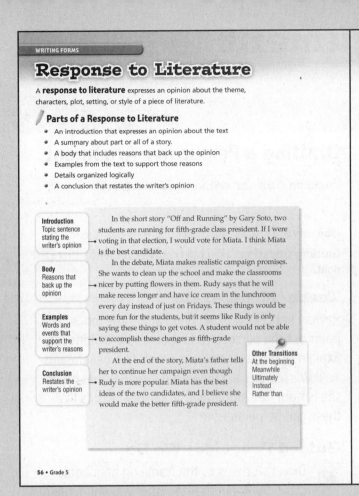

Introduction
Topic sentence stating the writer's opinion

In the short story "Off and Running" by Gary Soto, two students are running for fifth-grade class president. If I were voting in that election, I would vote for Miata. I think Miata is the best candidate.

Body
Reasons that back up the opinion

In the debate, Miata makes realistic campaign promises. She wants to clean up the school and make the classrooms nicer by putting flowers in them. Rudy says that he will make recess longer and have ice cream in the lunchroom every day instead of just on Fridays. These things would be more fun for the students, but it seems like Rudy is only saying these things to get votes. A student would not be able to accomplish these changes as fifth-grade president.

Examples
Words and events that support the writer's reasons

Conclusion
Restates the writer's opinion

At the end of the story, Miata's father tells her to continue her campaign even though Rudy is more popular. Miata has the best ideas of the two candidates, and I believe she would make the better fifth-grade president.

Other Transitions
At the beginning
Meanwhile
Ultimately
Instead
Rather than

Name _____

Follow your teacher's directions to complete this page.

1 Based on the details in the biography of James Forten by Walter Dean Myers, it is easy to see that the life of the child of free Africans in 1766 was very different from the lives of children living in America now.

First of all, _____

_____

_____ However, _____

_____

_____

_____ Most importantly, _____

Finally, _____

_____

2 On a separate sheet of paper, write a response to "The Birchbark House" by Louise Erdrich or another story you know. You might explain why you think the mother bear left Omakayas alone instead of attacking her.

3 On a separate sheet of paper, use your plan to write a response to literature, or make a new plan to respond to another story, such as "Storm Warriors" by Elisa Carbone. You might write about whether or not you think Nathan's father would have changed his mind about Nathan becoming a surfman.

Corrective Feedback

IF . . . students are having a hard time coming up with examples to support their opinions,

THEN . . . have them first think about possible objections to their opinions, and then find details that contrast with those statements. For example, if the opinion expressed is *I think Miata is the best candidate*, a possible objection might be *Miata doesn't have any good ideas*. Tell students that answering objections can be a good way to support an opinion. In this instance, the writer could answer the objection by writing *Miata has strong ideas, such as cleaning up the school.*

Focus Trait: Organization

Tell students that graphic organizers help them place their ideas where they will eventually be in the final written response. Explain that writers can use a variety of graphic organizers to organize a response to literature. A Venn diagram or T-chart, for example, work well for comparing and contrasting details. For responses that involve making an opinion statement, an idea-support map is useful.

Model various ways to organize supporting details in a response to literature. Have students suggest stories they have read and brainstorm opinion statements or opinion questions about the stories. Then, together, come up with suggestions for graphic organizers or writing plans best suited to each opinion statement or question. Tell students that there is often more than one graphic organizer that will be helpful to organize supporting details.

Persuasive Argument

Minilesson 45

Choosing Words for Purpose

Common Core State Standards: W.5.1b, W.5.1c

Objective: Choose words that persuade the reader.

Guiding Question: Which words will persuade the reader?

Teach/Model—I Do

Read aloud and discuss handbook p. 58. Explain that, when writers want to persuade readers, they choose words that will convince the reader to agree with them. Point out the reasons the writer includes in the second paragraph that back up his or her opinion. Help students identify words that help make those reasons sound persuasive—*wasted, for granted, wouldn't be so quick*, and so on. Discuss how this word choice convinces readers. Have students suggest other possible words that might help convince readers and write them on the board.

Guided Practice—We Do

On the board, write a suggestion for a school activity, such as *Our class should donate the clothes from the lost and found to a shelter* or *students should volunteer to read to younger kids.* Work with students to make a list of reasons why this would be a good idea. Guide them to think about persuasive words that would help make these reasons more convincing and circle them.

Practice/Apply—You Do

COLLABORATIVE Have students choose another idea from the list on the board. Have groups choose one action and write a list of persuasive words and phrases to support it.

INDEPENDENT Have students choose another action and write a list of persuasive words and phrases to support it.

Conference/Evaluate

Have students evaluate their lists to make sure their word choices are convincing to readers.

Minilesson 46

Drafting a Persuasive Argument

Common Core State Standards: W.5.1, W.5.4

Objective: Persuade the reader that your idea is right.

Guiding Question: How can I convince the reader that I am right?

Teach/Model—I Do

Review handbook p. 58. Read aloud the model and point out the persuasive language the writer uses. Explain that the writer uses words like *benefit* and *valuable lessons* to convince the reader that he or she is right. Tell students that positive words like these can be persuasive.

Guided Practice—We Do

 Direct students to the frame on handbook p. 59. Tell them that together you will write a persuasive argument about a committee to help students find volunteer opportunities. Work with students to write a list of reasons why this is a good idea. Then, together, complete the frame with reasons that include persuasive words, such as *First of all, volunteering helps the giver and the receiver.* Help students suggest word choices that are convincing. Have students write in their books as you write on the board.

Practice/Apply—You Do

 COLLABORATIVE Have groups plan and complete Activity 2. Tell them to choose positive words to persuade you. Have groups share what they have written.

 INDEPENDENT Have students read and follow the directions. Tell them to use their prewriting plan from Lesson 23 or to brainstorm a new plan using Graphic Organizer 7.

Conference/Evaluate

As students draft, have them evaluate their work using the rubric on p. 104.

Persuasive Argument

A **persuasive argument** expresses an opinion and tries to convince the reader to agree with that opinion.

Parts of a Persuasive Argument

- An introduction that clearly states the writer's opinion
- A body that gives reasons, facts, and examples to support that opinion
- Persuasive language to convince the reader
- A conclusion that summarizes the main argument

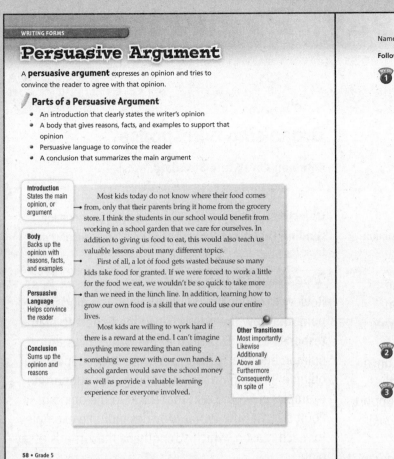

Introduction
States the main opinion, or argument

Body
Backs up the opinion with reasons, facts, and examples

Persuasive Language
Helps convince the reader

Conclusion
Sums up the opinion and reasons

Most kids today do not know where their food comes from, only that their parents bring it home from the grocery store. I think the students in our school would benefit from working in a school garden that we care for ourselves. In addition to giving us food to eat, this would also teach us valuable lessons about many different topics.

First of all, a lot of food gets wasted because so many kids take food for granted. If we were forced to work a little for the food we eat, we wouldn't be so quick to take more than we need in the lunch line. In addition, learning how to grow our own food is a skill that we could use our entire lives.

Most kids are willing to work hard if there is a reward at the end. I can't imagine anything more rewarding than eating something we grew with our own hands. A school garden would save the school money as well as provide a valuable learning experience for everyone involved.

Other Transitions
Most importantly
Likewise
Additionally
Above all
Furthermore
Consequently
In spite of

Name _____

Follow your teacher's directions to complete this page.

 1. Our school is not doing enough to encourage students to become involved in the community. The student council should start a committee to help students find ways to volunteer.

First of all, _____

_____

For instance, _____

_____

_____

_____

In addition, _____

_____

_____

_____

In order to _____

_____

_____

_____ become more involved

members of our community.

 2. On a separate sheet of paper, write a persuasive argument to convince your teacher to spend more time on your favorite subject.

3. On a separate sheet of paper, use your prewriting plan to write a persuasive argument, or make a new plan to write a persuasive argument to convince your readers to adopt a pet.

✓ Corrective Feedback

IF . . . students are having a hard time choosing persuasive words,

THEN . . . have them list pros and cons for their argument. Tell them to use the pros as persuasive reasons. For example, *The student council has too many committees* is a con, but *The committee can let students know who needs help* is a pro and a persuasive reason. Tell students that they can then add other words that make this benefit even more apparent. *(The committee can help by letting students know who needs volunteers.)*

Focus Trait: Organization

Tell students that they can choose words to persuade their readers by providing more than one reason why their argument is correct. Another trick to persuade readers is to refute a reason for disagreeing with the argument. Explain that writers persuade by making connections with the reader, and they often save the best and most beneficial reason for last. Model the process of organizing a list of reasons for students.

Make a list of reasons on the board. Have students read the list and order the reasons from least convincing to most convincing. Tell students that when writers choose reasons to convince the reader that they are right, they organize their reasons in the way they feel will be the most persuasive. The most convincing reasons are often the ones that tell the reader how the idea is beneficial to them.

Response Essay: Prewriting

Using Examples from the Text

Common Core State Standard: W.5.5

Objective: Use supporting examples from a text.

Guiding Question: What examples will support my opinion?

Teach/Model—I Do

Discuss handbook p. 60. Explain that a response essay is about a particular part of a text, such as theme, plot, etc. Point out the topic sentence, *Greg is a smart businessperson*, noting that this is the writer's opinion about the main character in "Lunch Money." The writer's plan includes reasons for that opinion, along with details from the text that support those reasons. On the board, write *His comic books could stand up on their own*. Discuss how this example supports the writer's reason, *He created an original product*.

Guided Practice—We Do

Discuss the story "Lunch Money" or another selection students have read. On the board, write an opinion sentence such as *Greg is a hard worker*. Work with students to write examples from the text that support this opinion. Help them find supporting examples, such as *He worked to draw a powerful cover illustration*.

Practice/Apply—You Do

COLLABORATIVE Have students choose another story and write an opinion statement about it. Have groups search the text for examples that support the opinion.

INDEPENDENT Have students write an opinion statement about the same story or choose a new story. Have them find examples from the text that support their opinion.

Conference/Evaluate

Have students evaluate their examples to make sure they support the reasons for the writer's opinion.

Organizing a Response

Common Core State Standard: W.5.5

Objective: Plan a response essay based on your opinion.

Guiding Question: What reasons and details support my topic?

Teach/Model—I Do

Review handbook p. 60. Read aloud the model and point out how the writer fills in the T-chart to plan a response essay. Explain that the writer gives an opinion and then provides reasons that support that opinion. In addition, the writer provides supporting examples from the text that back up the opinion. Point out that the writer provides multiple examples for each reason, which strengthens the writer's essay plan.

Guided Practice—We Do

 Direct students to Activity 1 on handbook p. 61. Tell them that, together, you will use a T-chart to plan a response essay. Work with students to brainstorm opinions about "Elisa's Diary." Help students complete the T-chart with reasons and examples from the text. Have students write in their books as you write on the board.

Practice/Apply—You Do

 COLLABORATIVE Have groups plan and complete Activity 2. Remind them to put reasons and details on their T-charts. Have groups share what they have written.

 INDEPENDENT Have students read and follow the directions. Tell them to use their prewriting plan from Lesson 24 or to brainstorm a new plan, using Graphic Organizer 12.

Conference/Evaluate

As students draft, have them evaluate their work using the rubric on p. 104.

 Digital
- eBook
- WriteSmart
- Interactive Lessons

Response Essay: Prewriting

A **response essay** is an essay that answers a question about any aspect of a text, such as theme, plot, or characters.

Parts of Prewriting for a Response Essay

- Brainstorm ideas about the story you have read
- Write down your opinion about an aspect of the story
- Using a T-map, write down reasons that support your opinion
- Write down details from the text to illustrate each reason

Topic: _Greg is a smart businessperson._

Reasons	Details
He created an original product.	• His comic books were short and sturdy, not tall and floppy. • His comics could stand up on their own.
He found something he could sell without getting in trouble.	• Candy and toys were against the rules. • He realized comic books were about reading.
He put a lot of effort into making his comics.	• Greg researched how to print his comics. • He planned the comics in the series before he wrote them.

Name _____

Follow your teacher's directions to complete this page.

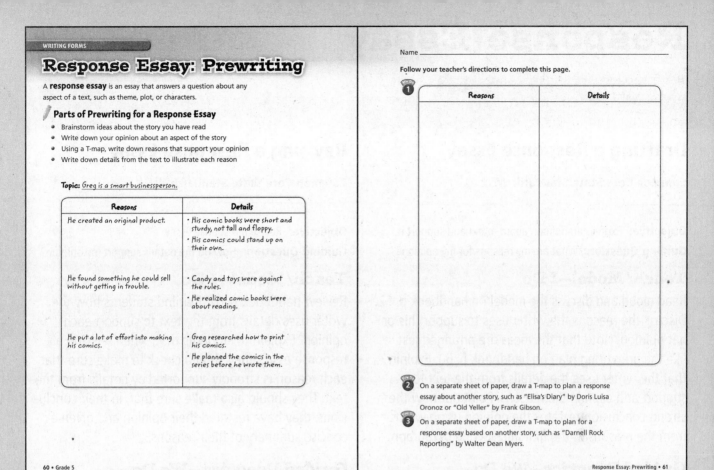

Reasons	Details

On a separate sheet of paper, draw a T-map to plan a response essay about another story, such as "Elisa's Diary" by Doris Luisa Oronoz or "Old Yeller" by Frank Gibson.

On a separate sheet of paper, draw a T-map to plan for a response essay based on another story, such as "Darnell Rock Reporting" by Walter Dean Myers.

Corrective Feedback

IF . . . students are having difficulty explaining their opinions,

THEN . . . remind them to use examples from the text as support for their ideas. Have students skim the text and highlight supporting details that relate to their main argument. Guide students to remove explanations that are not based on examples from the text.

Focus Trait: Organization

Tell students that, when they are making a prewriting plan, a graphic organizer such as a T-chart helps them keep their ideas in logical order. A response essay states an opinion and backs it up with several reasons for that opinion. A strong essay requires supporting details from the text that back up these reasons. Students can keep details for each reason organized next to the reason, which makes it easier for them to write well-organized paragraphs later.

Model writing an opinion about a simple story, such as a fairy tale, above a T-chart. Have students help you list three reasons that support that opinion, writing those reasons on the left hand side of the chart. Ask students to help complete the prewriting plan by providing two supporting details from the story for each reason. Remind them that the details have to come from the story, not from their imaginations.

Grade 5 • **61**

Response Essay

Minilesson 49

Drafting a Response Essay

Common Core State Standard: W.5.1

Objective: Express an opinion about a text and support it.

Guiding Question: What are my reasons for my opinion?

Teach/Model—I Do

Read aloud and discuss the model on handbook p. 62. Discuss the reasons the writer uses to support his or her opinion. Note that the ideas are arranged just like the prewriting plan on handbook p. 60. Explain that the writer uses the details from the text to support and explain the reasons. Point out how the strong conclusion restates the opinion using words from the reasons in the first and second paragraph.

Guided Practice—We Do

 Direct students to the frame on handbook p. 63. Tell students that, together, you will write a response essay about how two characters from "Elisa's Diary" (or another story) are different. Work with students to find examples from the text to support the opening statement. Have students write in their books as you write on the board.

Practice/Apply—You Do

 COLLABORATIVE Have groups plan and complete Activity 2. Tell them they can use a T-chart to plan their response essay. Have groups share what they have written.

 INDEPENDENT Have students read and follow the directions. Tell them to use their prewriting plan from Lesson 25 or to brainstorm a new plan using Graphic Organizer 12.

Conference/Evaluate

As students draft, have them evaluate their work using the rubric on p. 104.

Minilesson 50

Revising a Response Essay

Common Core State Standard: W.5.5

Objective: Revise a response essay.

Guiding Question: How do the details support my opinion?

Teach/Model—I Do

Review handbook p. 62. Remind students how the writer uses details from the text to support each opinion. Explain to students that, when revising a response essay, they should check to make sure that each reason is strongly supported by details from the text. They should also make sure that, in their conclusions, they have restated their opinion and given a concise summary of their reasons.

Guided Practice—We Do

Tell students that, together, you will revise the first response essay you drafted in Minilesson 49. Work with students to underline the reasons that support the opinion. Ask them if the reasons make sense and can be supported by details in the text. Help students suggest words that more strongly describe supporting details from the text. Have students write in their books as you write on the board.

Practice/Apply—You Do

COLLABORATIVE Have groups revise their essays from Activity 2 in Minilesson 49. Tell them to compare their prewriting plans with their essays to make their details are organized in a logical order. Have groups share their revised drafts.

INDEPENDENT Have students revise their essays from Activity 3 in Minilesson 49. Remind them to make sure that each of their opinions is supported by reasons and examples.

Conference/Evaluate

As students revise, circulate and assist them with their revisions if they need help.

 Digital
- eBook
- WriteSmart
- Interactive Lessons

Response Essay

A **response essay** is an essay that answers a question or shares an opinion about part of a text, such as theme, plot, or characters.

Parts of a Response Essay

- An introduction with a topic sentence that expresses an opinion about the text
- A body that includes reasons to support the opinion
- Specific examples from the text
- Details organized in a logical way
- A conclusion that restates the opinion in a strong, convincing way

Introduction Topic sentence	In the story "Lunch Money" by Andrew Clements, the main character is a student named Greg. Greg is a smart businessperson because he sells comic books at school and is very successful.
Body Reasons to support the opinion	Greg shows that he is smart by making a comic book that is different from other comics. Unlike comic books found in stores, Greg's comics are small, solid sixteen-page books that are easy to carry. The kids like the comics because they are unique.
Examples from the text	Greg knew that he had to find something that he could sell in school without getting in trouble. Because candy and toys were against the rules, Greg had to think of something else. He knew that comic books would be allowed because they encourage reading.
Conclusion Restates the opinion	In the story, Greg was not just lucky. By making a unique product and finding a way to sell something at school without getting into trouble, he made sure he would be successful. He showed that he was a smart businessperson.

Other Transitions
First of all
Rather than
As a result
However
Incidentally

Name _____

Follow your teacher's directions to complete this page.

1 In "Elisa's Diary" by Doris Luisa Oronoz, Elisa makes friends with another student named Jose. Elisa and Jose have a lot in common, but they are also different.

First of all, _____

_____

_____

In addition, _____

_____

_____

However, _____

_____

_____

_____ Instead of _____

At the end of the story, _____

_____

_____

2 On a separate sheet of paper, use your plan to write a response essay explaining why you think Elisa and her brother do not get along in "Elisa's Diary," or respond to a different story.

3 On a separate sheet of paper, use your prewriting plan to write a response essay about a story you have read, or use what you have learned to make a new plan.

Corrective Feedback

IF . . . students are having a hard time revising their response essays,

THEN . . . have them exchange essays with a peer, explaining that a second set of eyes often reveals mistakes that have been made. They can first tell each other if the reasons for holding the opinion in the topic sentence make sense and if the supporting details really back up the reasons. Then they can scan the text to make sure the supporting details are actually in the text.

Focus Trait: Word Choice

Tell students that word choice can make the difference between a strong response essay and a weak one. When writers choose details to support their reasons for holding an opinion, those details need to truly illustrate the reasons in a way that convinces readers that the opinion is correct.

Model creating strong supporting details for a text by first writing a weak version and then a strong version of the same detail. (For example, in regard to "Lunch Money," a weak detail would be that Greg makes a different kind of comic book; a strong detail would contrast the size, shape, and length of his comic book with those of other comic books.)

Have students read the two versions and decide which one is more convincing and better illustrates the reason. Remind them that when supporting their reasons for having an opinion about a text, they must explain those reasons with vivid details that actually occur in the text, rather than simply restating their opinion.

Grade 5 • **63**

Definition Paragraph

Minilesson 51

Using Clear Examples

Common Core State Standard: W.5.2b

Objective: Use clear examples to define a topic.

Guiding Question: Which examples clearly define my topic?

Teach/Model—I Do

Read aloud and discuss handbook p. 64. Explain that a definition paragraph should include facts, examples, and details that define the topic; they also should interest the reader. Point out the word *migrate* in the topic sentence and explain that the writer provides clear examples in the paragraph that define *monarch migration*. Explain that the writer of this paragraph has chosen details that not only are clear, but that also are unusual and interesting.

Guided Practice—We Do

On the board, draw a Four Square map. In the center of the map put a topic to define, such as *chameleons changing color*. Work with students to put details about that topic around the center of the map. With students, research those details using books or the Internet. Then fill in the map with interesting details that clearly explain the topic (for example, *Chameleons change color according to their mood*).

Practice/Apply—You Do

COLLABORATIVE Write several other topics to define, such as *seeing eye dogs*. Have groups choose one topic and fill in a Four Square map with clear examples that define the topic.

INDEPENDENT Have students choose another topic and fill in a Four Square map for it on their own.

Conference/Evaluate

Have students evaluate their maps to make sure they choose clear and interesting examples.

Minilesson 52

Drafting a Definition Paragraph

Common Core State Standard: W.5.2b

Objective: Choose facts and details for a definition paragraph.

Guiding Question: What facts and details will be the most interesting for my definition paragraph?

Teach/Model—I Do

Review handbook p. 64. Read aloud the model and point out the interesting facts and details that the writer uses to define the topic. Explain that the writer draws in the reader by choosing details that are remarkable or unusual. Point out that the last sentence of the definition paragraph sums up the main topic with a final detail.

Guided Practice—We Do

 Direct students to the frame on handbook p. 65. Tell them that together you will write a definition paragraph about their favorite animal. Work with students to write a sentence that states why the animal is a favorite. Then complete the frame with interesting and clear details. Have students write in their books as you write on the board.

Practice/Apply—You Do

 COLLABORATIVE Have groups plan and complete Activity 2. Tell them they can use the definition of *hibernation* to clarify their topic sentence. Have groups share what they have written.

 INDEPENDENT Have students read and follow the directions. Tell groups to use their prewriting plan from Lesson 26 or to brainstorm a new plan using Graphic Organizer 6.

Conference/Evaluate

As students draft, have them evaluate their work using the rubric on p. 104.

 Digital
- eBook
- WriteSmart
- Interactive Lessons

Definition Paragraph

A **definition paragraph** is a paragraph that explains one object or idea in detail.

Parts of a Definition Paragraph

- An introduction that names the object or idea to be defined
- Sentences that contain facts and examples to define the main topic
- Interesting details that engage the reader
- A logical organization of supporting details
- A closing sentence that summarizes the main idea

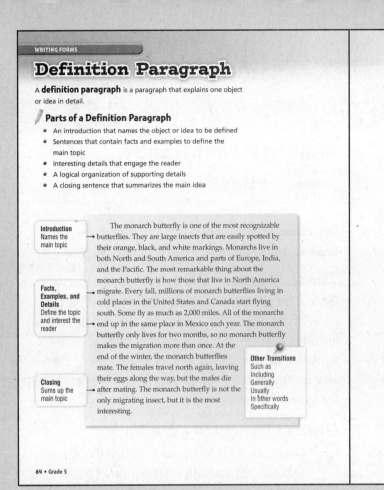

Introduction
Names the main topic

Facts, Examples, and Details
Define the topic and interest the reader

Closing
Sums up the main topic

The monarch butterfly is one of the most recognizable butterflies. They are large insects that are easily spotted by their orange, black, and white markings. Monarchs live in both North and South America and parts of Europe, India, and the Pacific. The most remarkable thing about the monarch butterfly is how those that live in North America migrate. Every fall, millions of monarch butterflies living in cold places in the United States and Canada start flying south. Some fly as much as 2,000 miles. All of the monarchs end up in the same place in Mexico each year. The monarch butterfly only lives for two months, so no monarch butterfly makes the migration more than once. At the end of the winter, the monarch butterflies mate. The females travel north again, leaving their eggs along the way, but the males die after mating. The monarch butterfly is not the only migrating insect, but it is the most interesting.

Other Transitions
Such as
Including
Generally
Usually
In other words
Specifically

Name _____

Follow your teacher's directions to complete this page.

My favorite animal is a _____
_____
_____

These animals are interesting because _____
_____

Unlike other animals, _____
_____
_____
_____

_____ For example, _____
_____

In other words, _____
_____
_____

In conclusion, _____
_____
_____

On a separate sheet of paper, write a definition paragraph about an animal that hibernates during the winter.

On a separate sheet of paper, use your prewriting plan to write a definition paragraph, or make a new plan to write a paragraph about an animal that is nocturnal, or active at night.

✔ Corrective Feedback

IF . . . students are having a hard time defining their topics,

THEN . . . encourage them to research facts and examples. Suggest that they use books or the Internet, making sure to paraphrase and cite their sources. Remind them to include only facts and examples that relate to the topic they are trying to define. Also suggest that they break their topic into smaller parts to make it easier to define.

Focus Trait: Word Choice

Tell students that, when they write a definition paragraph, they need to choose words to create a formal voice. To remind students of how the proper kind of formal voice sounds, read aloud or write the following on the board:

Monarch butterflies are so cool. I just love them.

Monarch butterflies, which migrate more than 2000 miles, have fascinated scientists and average people for many years.

Help students note that the first example not only expresses opinions, rather than just facts, but that it uses more informal words (such as *cool*). Explain that words like this are more appropriate for a conversation with a friend than for a formal piece of writing like a definition paragraph.

Ask students to suggest examples of inappropriately informal words or sentences and work together to revise them to sound more formal.

Journal Entry

Minilesson 53

Keeping a Journal

Common Core State Standards: W.5.2c, W.5.10

Objective: Use clear examples to define a topic.

Guiding Question: Which examples clearly define my topic?

Teach/Model—I Do

Read and discuss the model on p. 66. Tell students that a journal is a notebook or computer file that a writer uses to write about any topic. It includes the date and informal, unpolished language. Tell students that one way to use a journal is to keep track of what a writer is learning in school and what he would like to learn more about. Point out that the topic of the model journal entry is something the writer learned in school. Discuss how the writer talks about what he learned and what he'd like to find out more about.

Guided Practice—We Do

Work with students to set up a journal page by having them write in a notebook or a clean piece of paper. Start by guiding them to write the date at the top. Then help students suggest topics from science class, such as *marine animals* or *sea exploration*, to write a journal entry about. Work together to choose a topic and write the beginning of a journal entry that tells what the class learned about the topic and what else they are interested in learning about it.

Practice/Apply—You Do

COLLABORATIVE Have students work in groups to create journal entries. Have them choose a topic from the board and write a few sentences about what they know and want to learn.

INDEPENDENT Have students repeat the activity with another topic from the board.

Conference/Evaluate

Circulate and help students write their entries by prompting them to say what they like about the topic.

Minilesson 54

Drafting a Journal Entry

Common Core State Standard: W.5.2c

Objective: Write a journal entry.

Guiding Question: How do I write a journal entry?

Teach/Model—I Do

Review handbook p. 66 with students. Discuss the parts of a journal entry and point out that this model includes the date, a beginning that tells what the entry will be about, and interesting details. The writer also expresses his or her thoughts and feelings about the topic.

Guided Practice—We Do

 Direct students to Frame 1 on handbook p. 67. Explain that you will write a journal entry about a marine biology topic. Work together to choose a topic that the class is interested in, such as *coral reefs* or *deep sea fish*. Then guide students to write a journal entry telling what they like about the topic and what they'd like to learn more about, such as *I'm really interested in learning about unusual animals that live in coral reefs*. Have students write in their books as you write on the board.

Practice/Apply—You Do

 COLLABORATIVE Have groups plan and complete Frame 2 about a book they read recently. Remind them to include their thoughts and feelings about the book. Have groups share their work.

 INDEPENDENT Have students read and follow the directions. Remind them that a journal entry doesn't need polished writing and should include thoughts and feelings.

Conference/Evaluate

As students draft, have them evaluate their work using the rubric or the one on p. 104.

 Digital • eBook • WriteSmart • Interactive Lessons

Journal Entry

A **journal** is a notebook in which you can write about anything you want. You can write about things that happened to you or things that you learned.

Parts of a Journal Entry

- The date at the top of the page
- A beginning that tells what the entry is about
- Interesting and important details that show your thoughts and feelings
- Don't worry too much about spelling and grammar. You are expressing thoughts and ideas for future use.

> 10/1/12
>
> The Roanoke Colony is so cool! It has a really great mystery. How could a whole colony be lost? Historians still don't know what really happened at Roanoke, but our class is learning lots more about the colonies. I am really excited about our field trip to Colonial Williamsburg! Mom says I have an ancestor who lived in Virginia two hundred years ago! I want to learn more about how my ancestor lived.

Name _____

Follow your teacher's directions to complete this page.

 Science is my favorite class. I would like to learn more about marine biology.

I'm really interested in _____

_____
_____
_____
_____
_____
_____
_____

 I read a really great book last week. It was called _____

It was about _____

_____
_____
_____
_____
_____
_____

3 On a separate sheet of paper, write a journal entry about something interesting you learned this week.

Corrective Feedback

IF . . . students are unable to think of topics for their journal,

THEN . . . have them use a T-map or other graphic organizer to brainstorm a list of things they learned in school that they thought were interesting. In the left column, they can write topics they liked learning about. The items on the list can come from any subject area. In the right column, they can write either one more thing they would like to learn about the topic or something they didn't understand about it.

Focus Trait: Voice

Explain to students that they can give their journal entries a unique voice by including personal feelings and informal language. What this example on the board:

> I like airplanes, so I thought our study of the Wright Brothers was interesting. Who were other aviation pioneers?

Elicit from students how to give the entry a more personal voice. For example:

> Someday I want to be an airline pilot. That's why I loved learning about the Wright Brothers' first flight. Who were other inventors working on airplanes at the time?

Summary

Minilesson 55

Writing a Strong Topic Sentence

Common Core State Standard: W.5.2b

Objective: Write a strong topic sentence for a summary.
Guiding Question: What is the main topic of the text?

Teach/Model—I Do

Read aloud and discuss handbook p. 68. Explain that a strong topic sentence tells the reader what the text is about. Point out the topic sentence in the first paragraph, explaining that it states in simple, clear terms what the main idea of the text is about. The rest of the paragraph fills in details about the main topic. Then point out the ending, discussing how it restates the main topic and also gives some additional, interesting details.

Guided Practice—We Do

On the board, write the name of a well-known book, such as *Because of Winn-Dixie* or *My Side of the Mountain.* Work with students to write a strong topic sentence that introduces the book to the reader. Guide them to think about the answer to the question, "Who or what is this book about?"

Practice/Apply—You Do

COLLABORATIVE On the board, write several other titles of books students know well, such as *Bridge to Terabithia* or *The Cricket in Times Square.* Have groups choose one book and write a strong topic sentence that tells what the book is about.

INDEPENDENT Have students choose another book title and write a strong topic sentence on their own.

Conference/Evaluate

Have students evaluate their topic sentences to make sure they clearly state what the book is about.

Minilesson 56

Drafting a Summary

Common Core State Standard: W.5.2b

Objective: Write the most important main ideas from a text.
Guiding Question: How do I link together the most important ideas in a text?

Teach/Model—I Do

Review handbook p. 68. Read aloud the model and discuss the transitional words and phrases in the second and third paragraphs (*as a kid, after, later*). Explain how these words help show the time relationship between events. Point out that other transition words can show how ideas are linked in other ways, such as cause and effect (*as a result, because*) or comparison and contrast (*similar, unlike*). Remind students that they will need transition words like these in their own summaries.

Guided Practice—We Do

 Direct students to the frame on handbook p. 69. Tell students that, together, you will write a summary of "The Birchbark House" by Louise Eldrich. Work with students to write a topic sentence that states what the story is about. Then, together, complete the frame, using transitional words to link ideas and events. Have students write in their books as you write on the board.

Practice/Apply—You Do

 COLLABORATIVE Have groups plan and complete Activity 2, using transitional words to connect main ideas. Have groups share what they have written.

 INDEPENDENT Have students read and follow the directions. Tell them to use their prewriting plan from Lesson 28 or to make a new plan, using Graphic Organizer 4.

Conference/Evaluate

As students draft, have them evaluate their work using the rubric on p. 104

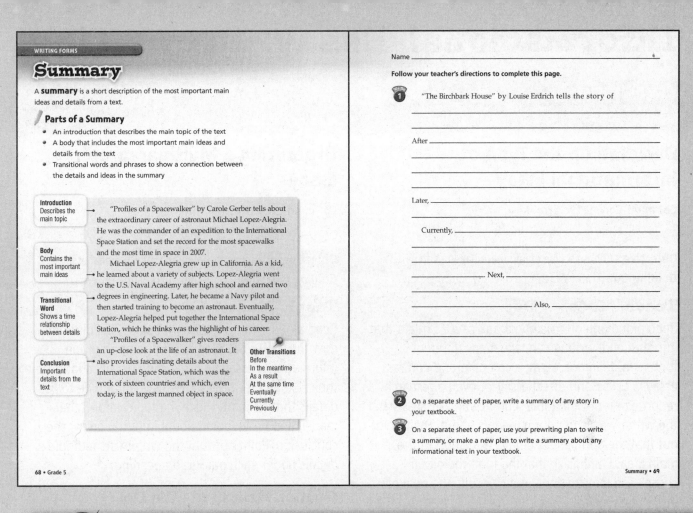

Summary

A **summary** is a short description of the most important main ideas and details from a text.

Parts of a Summary

- An introduction that describes the main topic of the text
- A body that includes the most important main ideas and details from the text
- Transitional words and phrases to show a connection between the details and ideas in the summary

Introduction
Describes the main topic

Body
Contains the most important main ideas

Transitional Word
Shows a time relationship between details

Conclusion
Important details from the text

"Profiles of a Spacewalker" by Carole Gerber tells about the extraordinary career of astronaut Michael Lopez-Alegria. He was the commander of an expedition to the International Space Station and set the record for the most spacewalks and the most time in space in 2007.

Michael Lopez-Alegria grew up in California. As a kid, he learned about a variety of subjects. Lopez-Alegria went to the U.S. Naval Academy after high school and earned two degrees in engineering. Later, he became a Navy pilot and then started training to become an astronaut. Eventually, Lopez-Alegria helped put together the International Space Station, which he thinks was the highlight of his career.

"Profiles of a Spacewalker" gives readers an up-close look at the life of an astronaut. It also provides fascinating details about the International Space Station, which was the work of sixteen countries and which, even today, is the largest manned object in space.

Other Transitions
Before
In the meantime
As a result
At the same time
Eventually
Currently
Previously

68 • Grade 5

Name _____

Follow your teacher's directions to complete this page.

 1   "The Birchbark House" by Louise Erdrich tells the story of

_____

_____

After _____

_____

_____

_____

Later, _____

_____

Currently, _____

_____

_____ Next, _____

_____ Also, _____

_____

_____

_____

_____

 2   On a separate sheet of paper, write a summary of any story in your textbook.

3   On a separate sheet of paper, use your prewriting plan to write a summary, or make a new plan to write a summary about any informational text in your textbook.

Summary • 69

✔ Corrective Feedback

IF . . . students are having a hard time coming up with a topic sentence,

THEN . . . have them start the sentence with the title of the text they are summarizing: For example, Diary of a Wimpy Kid *tells the story of* _____. Then have them revise the sentence to make it more interesting.

Focus Trait: Ideas

Tell students that, in a summary, it is important to connect main ideas in a logical way. If a text has events in time sequence, a timeline is a good way to organize important events or ideas in the order they occur in a text.

If the text is not time-directed, the ideas can be placed in order of importance. One way to tell which ideas are most important to an author of a text is to look at the topic sentences of each paragraph.

Another way to tell how ideas should be ordered is to see if the book has a table of contents or a list of chapter titles. Those titles can then be used as guides for main ideas.

Model organizing ideas for a summary using a flow chart or a timeline. Be sure to show students how to identify the important main ideas of a text using topic sentences, the table of contents, or chapter titles. Then help students fill in supporting details on the chart or time line.

Informational Essay: Prewriting

Minilesson 57

Deciding on the Type of Informational Essay

Common Core State Standard: W.5.2b

Objective: Choose a type of informational essay to write.

Guiding Question: Which type of essay suits my topic?

Teach/Model—I Do

Read aloud and discuss handbook p. 70. Explain that informational writing can take many different forms—a definition essay, a compare-and-contrast essay, a cause-and-effect essay, or even a research report. Point out the topic sentence and discuss what the writer wants to inform readers about. Then point out that the outline lists details that support the main idea. Emphasize that the form the writer chose—an informational essay—suits the goal of informing readers.

Guided Practice—We Do

On the board, brainstorm informational topics with students, such as *An unusual sport* or *How stars are formed.* Work with students to choose the type of informational writing best suited to the topic. Then guide them to suggest a graphic organizer to use for planning writing in that form.

Practice/Apply—You Do

COLLABORATIVE Have groups choose a topic from the list. Tell them to choose the type of writing they would use for the topic and to suggest a graphic organizer that would help plan their writing. Have them share their choices.

INDEPENDENT Have students choose another topic from the list and choose a writing form and an appropriate graphic organizer to fit the topic.

Conference/Evaluate

Have students evaluate their plans to make sure they suit the writing form they choose.

Minilesson 58

Organizing a Multiparagraph Essay

Common Core State Standard: W.5.5

Objective: Plan a multi-paragraph informational essay.

Guiding Question: How should I organize my essay?

Teach/Model—I Do

Read aloud and review handbook p. 70. Point out how the writer has planned a three-paragraph informational essay by organizing details about the topic. Explain that the writer uses an outline to list details that help introduce the topic, inform the reader, and provide additional information for the conclusion. Point out that the writer lists multiple details under each paragraph heading.

Guided Practice—We Do

 Direct students to Activity 1 on handbook p. 71. Tell them that, together, you will make an outline for an informational essay about a historical figure from your state. Work with students to brainstorm a topic sentence. Help students complete the outline with details for each paragraph heading. Have students write in their books as you write on the board.

Practice/Apply—You Do

 COLLABORATIVE Have groups plan and complete Activity 2. Remind them that their outlines should include an introduction, at least one paragraph, and a conclusion. Have groups share what they have written.

 INDEPENDENT Have students read and follow the directions. Tell them to use their prewriting plan from Lesson 29 or to brainstorm a new plan using an outline.

Conference/Evaluate

As students draft, have them evaluate their work using the rubric on p. 104.

 Digital
- eBook
- WriteSmart
- Interactive Lessons

Informational Essay: Prewriting

An **informational essay** explains a topic to the reader using facts. One way to plan an informational essay is to make an outline.

Parts of Prewriting for an Informational Essay

- Brainstorm topics that you want to tell readers about
- Decide on a main topic and write a topic sentence
- Make a list of details that support the main idea
- Take the details you listed and organize them into an outline that will guide you when you write your essay

Topic Sentence: *The Venus flytrap is an unusual plant.*

> I. Introduction: Venus Flytrap
>   A. Found in North and South Carolina
>   B. Lives in sunny and wet areas
>
> II. Eating Habits
>   A. Makes its own food using energy from the sun
>   B. Also eats small insects
>   C. Has leaves that trap prey
>   D. Takes a week to digest
>
> III. Conclusion
>   A. Most popular meat-eating plant
>   B. People take them out of the wild
>   C. More in homes and nurseries than in the wild

Name _____

Follow your teacher's directions to complete this page.

 1 Topic Sentence: _____

> I. Introduction: _____
>   A. _____
>   B. _____
>   C. _____
>
> II. The History of My State
>   A. _____
>   B. _____
>   C. _____
>
> III. Special Events in My State
>   A. _____
>   B. _____
>   C. _____
>
> IV. Conclusion
>   A. _____
>   B. _____
>   C. _____

 2 On a separate sheet of paper, plan an informational essay about an insect or plant that can be found where you live.

3 On a separate sheet of paper, plan an informational essay about a place you enjoy visiting.

Corrective Feedback

IF . . . students have difficulty deciding how to organize their informational essay,

THEN . . . have them first list details about the topic and then use the details to help them decide how to organize. For example, for the topic *How stars are formed*, they might organize their details by causes and effects.

Focus Trait: Organization

Tell students that, when they are making a prewriting plan for an informational essay, an idea-support map works well for organizing each paragraph in outline form. However, it is also possible to start the prewriting process with other graphic organizers, such as information webs. This helps students brainstorm ideas for what types of information they want to write about. Then they can choose what type of approach they want to take with their essays.

Once students know the aspect of their topic that will be their focus, they can use an outline to create paragraph headings and fill in supporting details.

Model brainstorming an information web graphic organizer with students, using a one-word topic. Ask students to continue developing the prewriting plan by choosing one aspect of the topic to research for further details. Then have students start an outline for their prewriting plan, creating paragraph headings for their chosen topic focus.

Grade 5 • **71**

Informational Essay

Drafting an Informational Essay

Common Core State Standard: W.5.2b

Objective: Explain a topic using informative details.

Guiding Question: What information should I use to explain my topic?

Teach/Model—I Do

Read aloud and discuss handbook p. 72. Point out the topic sentence in the introductory paragraph. Explain that the writer uses details to support the main idea expressed in the topic sentence. The writer organizes details and facts according to the prewriting plan on handbook p. 70. The conclusion ties together details that support the topic sentence.

Guided Practice—We Do

 Direct students to the frame on handbook p. 73. Tell students that, together, you will write an informational essay about an important person in the state's history, using their plan from Lesson 29. Work with students to write a topic sentence that explains why the person was important and complete the frame with details that support the topic sentence. Have students write in their books as you write on the board.

Practice/Apply—You Do

 COLLABORATIVE Have groups use their plans from the previous lesson or make a new plan and write an informational essay. Have groups share what they have written.

 INDEPENDENT Have students use their prewriting plan from the previous lesson or brainstorm a new plan using an outline.

Conference/Evaluate

As students draft, have them evaluate their work using the rubric on p. 104.

Revising an Informational Essay

Common Core State Standard: W.5.2b

Objective: Revise an informational essay.

Guiding Question: Are my supporting details organized?

Teach/Model—I Do

Review handbook p. 72. Explain that the details the writer used expanded on the topic sentence and gave the reader additional information about the topic. Point out that, when revising a response essay, writers should make sure that the details support both their overall topic sentence and the main ideas of their paragraphs. They should also make sure that they have a conclusion that ties together details.

Guided Practice—We Do

Have students turn to the completed frame on handbook p. 73. Ask them if the supporting details are logically organized. Help students suggest details that more strongly support the main idea or better organize the information. Have students write in their books as you write on the board. Encourage them to add or delete details when necessary.

Practice/Apply—You Do

COLLABORATIVE Have groups work together to revise their essays from Activity 2 in Minilesson 59. Remind students to look for how well their details are organized and if they have enough details to support their topic. Have them add or delete details as needed.

INDEPENDENT Have students revise their essays from Activity 3 in Minilesson 59. Tell them to make sure they have enough details to support their topic and that the details are organized in a logical way.

Conference/Evaluate

As students revise, circulate and assist them with their revisions if they need help.

 Digital
- eBook
- WriteSmart
- Interactive Lessons

Informational Essay

An **informational essay** explains a topic to the reader using facts.

Parts of an Informational Essay

- An introduction paragraph that includes a topic sentence
- Body paragraphs with details that support the main idea
- Details and facts presented in a logical order
- A conclusion that sums up the essay

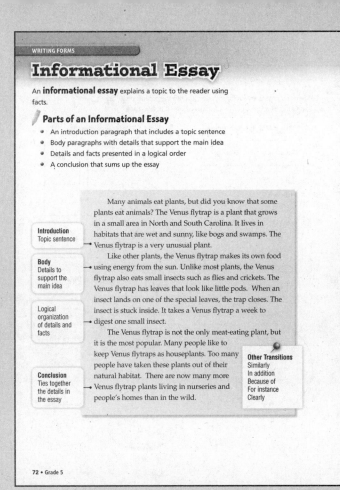

Introduction
Topic sentence

Body
Details to support the main idea

Logical organization of details and facts

Conclusion
Ties together the details in the essay

Many animals eat plants, but did you know that some plants eat animals? The Venus flytrap is a plant that grows in a small area in North and South Carolina. It lives in habitats that are wet and sunny, like bogs and swamps. The Venus flytrap is a very unusual plant.

Like other plants, the Venus flytrap makes its own food using energy from the sun. Unlike most plants, the Venus flytrap also eats small insects such as flies and crickets. The Venus flytrap has leaves that look like little pods. When an insect lands on one of the special leaves, the trap closes. The insect is stuck inside. It takes a Venus flytrap a week to digest one small insect.

The Venus flytrap is not the only meat-eating plant, but it is the most popular. Many people like to keep Venus flytraps as houseplants. Too many people have taken these plants out of their natural habitat. There are now many more Venus flytrap plants living in nurseries and people's homes than in the wild.

Other Transitions
Similarly
In addition
Because of
For instance
Clearly

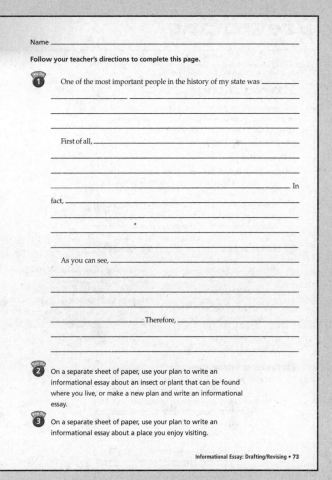

Name _____

Follow your teacher's directions to complete this page.

1 One of the most important people in the history of my state was _____

_____

_____

First of all, _____

_____

_____

_____ In

fact, _____

_____

_____

As you can see, _____

_____

_____

_____ Therefore, _____

_____

2 On a separate sheet of paper, use your plan to write an informational essay about an insect or plant that can be found where you live, or make a new plan and write an informational essay.

3 On a separate sheet of paper, use your plan to write an informational essay about a place you enjoy visiting.

Corrective Feedback

IF . . . students are having a hard time organizing the information for their essays,

THEN . . . have them switch essays with a peer. Explain that a second set of eyes often reveals where changes need to be made. First have the student pairs determine if the organization of details in each essay makes sense. Then have them see if there are enough details supporting the main topic or if there are unnecessary details that should be deleted.

Focus Trait: Ideas

Tell students that a topic sentence is a promise to deliver information about a topic. Sometimes there is so much information available on a topic that writers can get overwhelmed. Tell them that this is why it is important to narrow their ideas to something more specific and not choose to write about something too broad. In this way, they can write a solid, clear topic sentence that tells the reader the kind of information that will follow in the rest of the essay.

Model writing a topic sentence about a specific topic, such as *The ibis is a common bird in Florida.* Then write a topic sentence with a broad topic, such as *Florida has many kinds of birds.* Have students read the two and decide which one will lead to a clear and informative essay. Discuss why the first topic sentence is better.

Grade 5 • 73

Prewriting

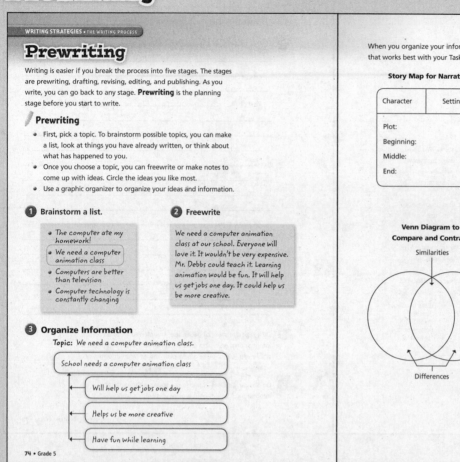

Prewriting

Writing is easier if you break the process into five stages. The stages are prewriting, drafting, revising, editing, and publishing. As you write, you can go back to any stage. **Prewriting** is the planning stage before you start to write.

Prewriting

- First, pick a topic. To brainstorm possible topics, you can make a list, look at things you have already written, or think about what has happened to you.
- Once you choose a topic, you can freewrite or make notes to come up with ideas. Circle the ideas you like most.
- Use a graphic organizer to organize your ideas and information.

1 Brainstorm a list.

- The computer ate my homework!
- We need a computer animation class
- Computers are better than television
- Computer technology is constantly changing

2 Freewrite

We need a computer animation class at our school. Everyone will love it. It wouldn't be very expensive. Mr. Debbs could teach it. Learning animation would be fun. It will help us get jobs one day. It could help us be more creative.

3 Organize Information

Topic: We need a computer animation class.

School needs a computer animation class

Will help us get jobs one day

Helps us be more creative

Have fun while learning

74 • Grade 5

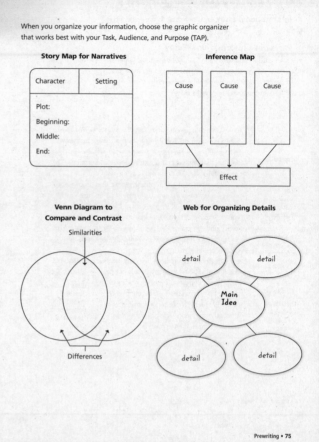

When you organize your information, choose the graphic organizer that works best with your Task, Audience, and Purpose (TAP).

Story Map for Narratives

Character | Setting
Plot:
Beginning:
Middle:
End:

Inference Map

Cause | Cause | Cause
Effect

Venn Diagram to Compare and Contrast

Similarities
Differences

Web for Organizing Details

detail | detail
Main Idea
detail | detail

Prewriting • 75

WRITING STRATEGY

Minilesson 61

Introducing Prewriting

Common Core State Standard: W.5.5

Objective: Understand how to use the information about prewriting that is presented in this lesson.

Guiding Question: How can I use these pages to help me plan my writing?

Teach/Model

Have students read page 74. Explain that the example shows how writers can brainstorm topics, come up with ideas, and organize their ideas and information.

Practice/Apply

Have students practice brainstorming an idea for writing. Encourage them to make a list, freewrite, and use a graphic organizer to make a plan.

Minilesson 62

Choosing a Graphic Organizer

Common Core State Standard: W.5.5

Objective: Understand how to choose the right graphic organizer for a prewriting plan.

Guiding Question: How do I choose a graphic organizer?

Teach/Model

Explain to students that each graphic organizer writers use depends on the task, audience, and purpose of their writing. Discuss how this writer chose a prewriting plan for a persuasive essay. Note how the details appear in the same order as they will in the essay.

Practice/Apply

Have students discuss why each graphic organizer on p. 75 was chosen for each type of writing.

Drafting

WRITING STRATEGIES • THE WRITING PROCESS

Drafting

Drafting is the second step of the writing process. When you draft, you use your prewriting plan to write what you planned.

Drafting

Sometimes your graphic organizer already has all the information you need for your draft. Turn your main ideas and details into complete, clear sentences.

At other times, you may need to elaborate ideas further. As you draft, add extra details or ideas not in the graphic organizer.

Persuasive Essay

Topic: We need a computer animation class.

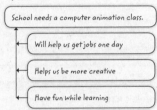

School needs a computer animation class.

Will help us get jobs one day

Helps us be more creative

Have fun while learning

Draft

A computer animation class will help us. People who make movies, cartoons, and video games need these classes. Mr. Debbs could teach it. Even jobs that didn't use animation before use it now. For example, people who write for newspapers now add animated things to their articles on the Internet. We never know if our jobs will need us to learn these skills.

The drafting stage is sometimes called *writing a first draft*. In this stage, put your ideas into complete sentences and add more ideas as they come to you. Don't worry if your draft is not quite right yet. You can make changes and fix mistakes at a later stage.

Fictional Narrative

Topic: "The computer ate my homework!"

teacher	Patricia
concerned, asks for homework doesn't believe Patricia	"You won't believe it: the computer ate it." She is a little afraid. tries to convince teacher

Draft

"Patricia, where is your homework?" Ms. Burns asked. She frowned slightly. "You are not usually late with it."

"You'll never believe me!" Patricia cried. "The computer ate it!" She was a little afraid of what would happen.

"Now I've heard everything," Ms. Burns said.

"It's true," said Patricia. "A big mouth appeared on the screen!"

Ms. Burns frowned. "I've never heard of anything like that before."

WRITING STRATEGY

Minilesson 63

Introducing Drafting

Common Core State Standard: W.5.5

Objective: Understand how to use the information about drafting that is presented in this lesson.

Guiding Question: How can I use these pages to help me start a draft?

Teach/Model

Have students read page 76. Explain that the example shows how a student used the graphic organizer to create a prewriting plan and then to write a first draft for a persuasive essay.

Practice/Apply

Have students read the example on p. 77. Discuss how the example shows a different type of plan, and point out how the student used it to write a first draft.

Minilesson 64

Using Your Organizer to Draft

Common Core State Standard: W.5.5

Objective: Understand how to use a graphic organizer to draft.

Guiding Question: How do I use my prewriting plan to draft?

Teach/Model

Explain to students that their prewriting plans give them a logical structure for the first draft. They write the ideas from the plan in complete sentences, using the same order. Then they fill in more details as they go along. Remind students that they will revise and edit their drafts later.

Practice/Apply

Have students discuss how the writer used information from each graphic organizer to start each draft with the main idea. The writer then filled in more details.

Revising

WRITING STRATEGIES • THE WRITING PROCESS

Revising

Revising is the third stage in the writing process. When you revise, you improve your draft.

Revising
- Make sure your main ideas are clear.
- Take out information that does not support your topic or main idea. Add details that better support your topic or main ideas.
- Reorganize sentences to create a clear, logical order.
- Make sure your words and information are specific.
- Add transition words and phrases if necessary.

Ways to Revise
- Use editor's marks to show your revisions.
- Add words, sentences, or paragraphs.

Editor's Marks
≡ Make a capital.
∧ Insert.
⌫ Delete.
⊙ Make a period.
⌃ Insert a comma.
/ Make lowercase.

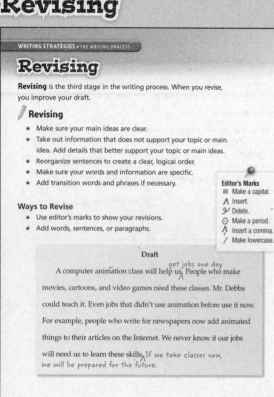

Draft

A computer animation class will help us. *get jobs one day* People who make movies, cartoons, and video games need these classes. Mr. Debbs could teach it. Even jobs that didn't use animation before use it now. For example, people who write for newspapers now add animated things to their articles on the Internet. We never know if our jobs will need us to learn these skills. *If we take classes now, we will be prepared for the future.*

- Cut out words or sentences you don't need.

Draft

A computer animation class will help us. *gets jobs one day* People who make movies, cartoons, and video games need these classes. ~~Mr. Debbs could teach it.~~ Even jobs that didn't use animation before use it now. For example, people who write for newspapers now add animated things to their articles on the Internet. We never know if our jobs will need us to learn these skills. *If we take classes now, we will be prepared for the future.*

- Add information to make your writing more specific

Draft

A computer animation class will help us. *gets jobs one day* People who make movies, cartoons, and video games need these classes. ~~Mr. Debbs could teach it.~~ Even jobs that didn't use animation before use it now. For example, people who write for newspapers now add *moving maps, charts, and pictures* ~~animated things~~ to their articles on the Internet. We never know if our jobs will need us to learn these skills. *If we take classes now, we will be prepared for the future.*

78 • Grade 5

Revising • 79

WRITING STRATEGY

Minilesson 65

Introducing Revising

Common Core State Standard: W.5.5

Objective: Understand how to use the information about revising that is presented in this lesson.

Guiding Question: How can I use these pages to help me revise my draft?

Teach/Model

Have students read page 78. Explain that the example on this page shows how a student added more details to support the main idea of the draft.

Practice/Apply

Have students read the examples on p. 79. Discuss how the student took out a sentence that did not support the main idea and made the idea clearer by adding another specific detail.

Minilesson 66

Revising Your Draft

Common Core State Standard: W.5.5

Objective: Understand different ways to revise a first draft.

Guiding Question: How should I revise to improve my draft?

Teach/Model

Explain that the revision process includes taking out ideas that don't support the main topic and adding details that clarify ideas and better support the topic. Writers add words, sentences, or paragraphs that give more specific information and cut what they don't need. Then they reorganize the information for clarity.

Practice/Apply

Have students practice revising a draft of their own by removing unnecessary details, adding more specific information, and reorganizing information.

Editing and Publishing

Editing

Editing is the stage of the writing process that often follows revising. During this stage, you proofread for any errors you may have made.

Editing

- Check for and correct any mistakes in punctuation, capitalization, spelling, and grammar.
- Make sure all your sentences are complete and correct. Check for run-on sentences or fragments. Also, make sure your subjects and verbs agree.
- If you edit on paper, use editor's marks.
- If you edit on the computer, use the spelling and grammar checker. Double-check your work. The computer does not catch everything.

Editor's Marks
≡ Make a capital.
∧ Insert.
⌫ Delete.
⊙ Make a period.
∧ Insert a comma.
/ Make lowercase.

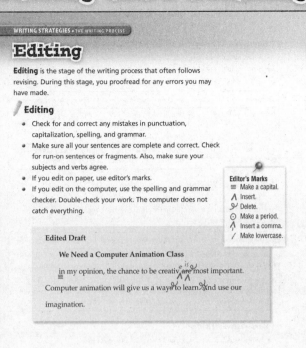

Edited Draft

We Need a Computer Animation Class

in my opinion, the chance to be creative are most important.

Computer animation will give us a ways to learn and use our imagination.

Publishing

Publishing is the final step of the writing process. When you publish, you share your writing with others.

Publishing

- When you publish, you prepare a final version of your writing to present to an audience.
- The final product can be a speech or oral presentation, a poster or visual presentation, or a printed item. You can use a computer or your best handwriting to make a final copy. You may want to include graphics, such as drawings or charts.
- You can create a portfolio of writing you want to save.

Our School Needs Computer Animation Now!
By Alexander Rothstein

A computer animation class might help us get jobs one day. People who make movies, cartoons, and video games need these classes. Even jobs that didn't use animation before use it now. For example, people who write for newspapers now add moving maps, charts, and pictures to their articles on the Internet. We don't know for certain yet if our jobs will need us to learn these skills. However, if we take classes now, we will be prepared for the future.

WRITING STRATEGY

Minilesson 67

Understanding the Editing Process

Common Core State Standard: W.5.5

Objective: Understand how to use the information about editing that is presented in this lesson.

Guiding Question: How can I use this page to edit a draft?

Teach/Model

Have students read page 80. Explain that the example on this page shows how a student used editor's marks to correct errors in the draft. Remind students that they have to check their drafts carefully because computer spell-checkers do not catch everything.

Practice/Apply

Discuss the errors that the writer found, as well as how he used editor's marks to correct them. Have students edit their own sample draft.

Minilesson 68

Understanding the Publishing Process

Common Core State Standard: W.5.5

Objective: Understand how to use the information presented in this lesson to publish a final product.

Guiding Question: How should I share the final version of my writing?

Teach/Model

Have students read page 81. Explain that publishing means presenting writing in its final form to an audience; there are many ways to publish, including saving writing in a portfolio.

Practice/Apply

Have students discuss why the student presented his essay as a printed piece. Have them suggest others ways he could have published the piece.

Ideas

Ideas

Writing traits are the qualities found in all good writing. The six writing traits are **ideas**, organization, word choice, voice, sentence fluency, and conventions. Ideas are the thoughts that you will convey through your writing.

Ideas

- Brainstorm several possible topic ideas and select the one you will write about. Make sure your topic is narrow, or specific, enough to cover in one piece of writing.
- Write all your ideas about your topic in a list. Select two or three main ideas to focus on.
- Get rid of ideas that do not fit your topic.
- Organize your ideas in a graphic organizer.

Preparing for a tornado
locate fastest, safest area to hide in
gather necessities: food, radio, flashlight
follow emergency instructions
move quickly to safe spot, and wait until you hear it's safe to come out

Narrative Writing

- Think about characters, plot, and setting.
- Good graphic organizers to use for ideas: story map, 5 Ws chart, column chart

Character	My Own Experience	Inference About Character
James likes to travel.	I enjoy taking trips. They are fun and exciting. They feel like adventures.	James is adventurous.
Sergio, James's dog, travels with James.	My dog Ralph is friendly and likes to go for walks.	Sergio is easy-going and a good companion.

Informative Writing

- Make a list of details and questions about a topic.
- Good graphic organizers to use for ideas: flow chart, note cards, KWL chart

K – What I Know	W – What I Want to Know	L – What I Have Learned
1. Scientists are studying if there could be life on Mars.	1. What new technology are scientists using to explore Mars?	1. The newest Mars Rover is called "Curiosity"
2. They send robots to gather data. The robots are called Mars Rovers.	2. How can they tell if there is or was life on Mars?	2. Scientists look for evidence that there was water on Mars.

Persuasive Writing

- Write your goal or opinion, and then think of and research reasons, facts, and examples.
- Possible graphic organizers for ideas: idea-support map, column chart, T-map

Opinion	Reasons
Hockey is the best sport.	-- It requires skill to skate and swing a hockey stick -- It's fast and fun. -- You can play outside in the winter or inside year round.

WRITING STRATEGY

Minilesson 69

Introducing Ideas

Common Core State Standard: W.5.4

Objective: Understand how to use the information about ideas that is presented in this lesson.

Guiding Question: How can I use these pages to help me organize my ideas?

Teach/Model

Have students read p. 82. Explain that the example on this page shows how a student used a flowchart to organize a list of ideas about a topic.

Practice/Apply

Have students read the examples on p. 83. Discuss the kinds of ideas that are best to think about for each type of writing. Also discuss how those ideas are organized in each graphic organizer.

Minilesson 70

Developing and Organizing Ideas

Common Core State Standard: W.5.4

Objective: Understand how to develop and organize ideas.

Guiding Question: How do I get ideas for my topic and organize them?

Teach/Model

Explain that, once writers have brainstormed for ideas, they need to narrow down how many ideas they use for a topic, keeping only the ones that support that topic well. Remind students that they can clarify their ideas once they plug them into a graphic organizer.

Practice/Apply

Have students brainstorm ideas for a fictional story, a personal narrative, or a piece of informative or persuasive writing, using one of the organizers.

Organization

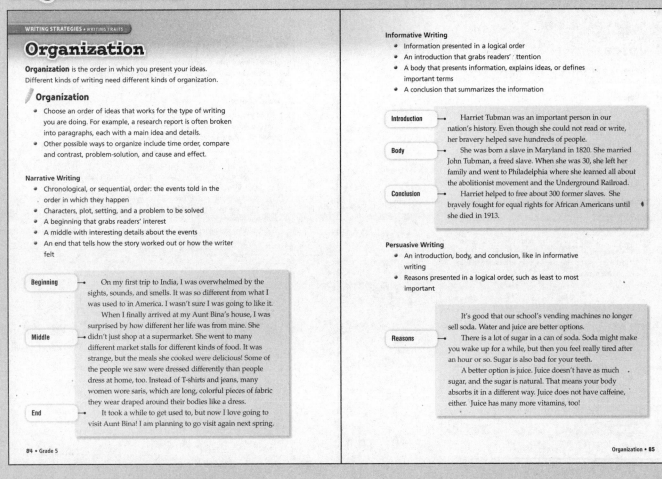

WRITING STRATEGIES • WRITING TRAITS

Organization

Organization is the order in which you present your ideas. Different kinds of writing need different kinds of organization.

Organization
- Choose an order of ideas that works for the type of writing you are doing. For example, a research report is often broken into paragraphs, each with a main idea and details.
- Other possible ways to organize include time order, compare and contrast, problem-solution, and cause and effect.

Narrative Writing
- Chronological, or sequential, order: the events told in the order in which they happen
- Characters, plot, setting, and a problem to be solved
- A beginning that grabs readers' interest
- A middle with interesting details about the events
- An end that tells how the story worked out or how the writer felt

Beginning → On my first trip to India, I was overwhelmed by the sights, sounds, and smells. It was so different from what I was used to in America. I wasn't sure I was going to like it.

Middle → When I finally arrived at my Aunt Bina's house, I was surprised by how different her life was from mine. She didn't just shop at a supermarket. She went to many different market stalls for different kinds of food. It was strange, but the meals she cooked were delicious! Some of the people we saw were dressed differently than people dress at home, too. Instead of T-shirts and jeans, many women wore saris, which are long, colorful pieces of fabric they wear draped around their bodies like a dress.

End → It took a while to get used to, but now I love going to visit Aunt Bina! I am planning to go visit again next spring.

84 • Grade 5

Informative Writing
- Information presented in a logical order
- An introduction that grabs readers' attention
- A body that presents information, explains ideas, or defines important terms
- A conclusion that summarizes the information

Introduction → Harriet Tubman was an important person in our nation's history. Even though she could not read or write, her bravery helped save hundreds of people.

Body → She was born a slave in Maryland in 1820. She married John Tubman, a freed slave. When she was 30, she left her family and went to Philadelphia where she learned all about the abolitionist movement and the Underground Railroad.

Conclusion → Harriet helped to free about 300 former slaves. She bravely fought for equal rights for African Americans until she died in 1913.

Persuasive Writing
- An introduction, body, and conclusion, like in informative writing
- Reasons presented in a logical order, such as least to most important

Reasons → It's good that our school's vending machines no longer sell soda. Water and juice are better options.
There is a lot of sugar in a can of soda. Soda might make you wake up for a while, but then you feel really tired after an hour or so. Sugar is also bad for your teeth.
A better option is juice. Juice doesn't have as much sugar, and the sugar is natural. That means your body absorbs it in a different way. Juice does not have caffeine, either. Juice has many more vitamins, too!

Organization • 85

WRITING STRATEGY

Minilesson 71

Introducing Organization

Common Core State Standard: W.5.4

Objective: Understand how to use the information about organization that is presented in this lesson.

Guiding Question: How can I use these pages to help me present my ideas in the correct order?

Teach/Model

Have students read p. 84. Explain that this example shows how a student organized events in a personal narrative, using a beginning, middle, and ending.

Practice/Apply

Have students identify and list the events in the beginning, middle, and end of the narrative on p. 84. Have them decide whether the example fulfills the requirements listed in the bulleted points above.

Minilesson 72

Organizing Ideas

Common Core State Standard: W.5.4

Objective: Understand how different types of writing require different kinds of organization.

Guiding Question: What type of organization should I use?

Teach/Model

Explain that different types of writing require different orders of ideas. Point out that the logical order of ideas depends on the goal of the writing (for example, narrative writing often uses time order).

Practice/Apply

Have students read the examples on p. 85. Have them make a Venn diagram comparing and contrasting the organization of informative and persuasive pieces.

Voice and Word Choice

Voice

Your **voice** and **word choice** affect your readers. Voice is a writer's unique way of saying things.

Voice

- A writer's voice lets the audience know what the writer is like.
- It sets the tone, or overall feeling, of the piece of writing. The tone shows how the writer feels about a topic.
- Match your voice with your purpose. A narrative voice should sound personal or natural. An informative voice should sound well-informed and less personal. A persuasive voice should sound convincing and positive.

Informal Voice: Use for friendly letters and personal narratives.

> Dear Penny,
>
> I can't wait to go to camp! It will be so cool to have you as a bunk mate. We'll get to do lots of hiking and boating. I'm so lucky to have my BFF going to camp with me!
>
> Love,
> Lila

Formal Voice: Use for business letters, informative writing, reports, and instructions.

> When the moon travels around the Earth, we can see the brighter parts of its surface reflected at different angles. These bright parts are commonly known as "phases" of the Moon. Each phase of the moon depends upon its position to the Sun and the Earth.

Word Choice

Good **word choice** helps paint a clear picture for readers. It helps describe characters, settings, and actions. Replace unclear words with words that are more exact.

Word Choice

- Good word choice creates a picture in the reader's mind.
- Precise words help readers know just what you mean. For example, *carrots* is a more precise, or exact, word than *food*.

> **First Draft**
> Maria and I could not get the thing to fly. Each time we tried, the wind stopped. Maria tried running one way. I tried running the other. Still, we could not get it off the ground.
> "Let's try one more time," Maria said. She pointed at something.
> We went up a hill. This time a strong wind lifted the kite into the sky. Maria shouted. We flew the kite until later.

> **Draft Revised for Word Choice**
> My sister Maria and I could not get the kite to fly. Each time we tried, the wind stopped. Maria tried running to the left. I tried running to the right. Still, we could not get the kite off the ground.
> "Let's try one more time," Maria said. She pointed at a hill in the distance.
> We climbed up the hill. This time a strong wind lifted the kite into the sky. Maria cheered and jumped up and down. We flew the kite until the sun began to set.

Minilesson 73

Understanding Voice

Common Core State Standard: W.5.4

Objective: Understand how to use the information about voice that is presented in this lesson.

Guiding Question: How can I use this page to help me match my voice to my purpose?

Teach/Model

Have students read p. 86. Explain that the examples on this page show the differences between informal and formal voice.

Practice/Apply

Have students discuss the ways that voice changes with the purpose of the writing. Have them identify the voice a writer would use for specific audiences and purposes (formal voice for a letter to the mayor, informal voice for a short story written for friends.)

Minilesson 74

Understanding Word Choice

Common Core State Standard: W.5.4

Objective: Understand how to use the information on word choice presented in this lesson.

Guiding Question: How can I use this page to help me choose the right words to express my ideas?

Teach/Model

Have students read p. 87. Explain that the examples show how a student revised a draft for word choice, changing words to ones that are more precise.

Practice/Apply

Have students discuss the word choice changes. Note how the changes help give the reader a clearer picture of events. Ask students to suggest other word choice changes the student could have made.

Sentence Fluency

Sentence Fluency

Writing traits are the qualities found in all good writing. Checking your **sentence fluency** will help your writing flow smoothly for readers.

Sentence Fluency

- Use a mix of long and short sentences.
- Vary the way sentences begin. You don't always have to start with the subject. You can also start with transition words or phrases.
- Use a variety of sentence types, like questions, statements, and exclamations.
- Read aloud your writing to hear how it flows.

Revise choppy sentences to be smoother.

Choppy Sentences	Smooth Sentences
Chantal wanted to explore caves. She needed training. Chantal knew that. But she had to take a class. The class taught her the safety rules. You needed a certificate to explore them. The park rangers would not let her do it. So Chantal took the class. She worked hard. She earned her certification. She was sure to bring a camera when she went on her first cave exploration trip.	All her life, Chantal wanted to explore caves. She also knew she had to train and take a class on safety rules before she could do it. Without the proper certificate, the park rangers wouldn't let her explore the caves. So Chantal took the class. She worked hard and got her certification. On her first cave exploration trip, she was sure to bring a camera.

Combine choppy sentences into longer, smoother ones.

Choppy Sentences	Longer, Smoother Sentences
The yard needed to be raked. The yard was covered with leaves.	The yard needed to be raked because it was covered with leaves.
A squirrel dug up the garden. He dug up carrots, lettuce, and peppers.	A squirrel came to the garden and dug up the carrots, lettuce, and peppers.

Use a variety of sentence beginnings.

Too Many Sentences Beginning the Same Way	Varied Beginnings
Sean wanted the part. Sean knew he was perfect for the role. He had practiced the lines all day. He practiced the lines while looking in the mirror. He said, "I will get this part."	Sean wanted the part and knew he was perfect for the role. He practiced the lines all day. While practicing in the mirror, he said aloud to himself, "I will get this part!"

Use different sentence lengths and kinds of sentences.

Too Many Sentences of the Same Length and Type	Varied Lengths and Types
Baking soda can be used for many purposes. You can mix it with water and use it to relieve insect bites. It can be used to remove scuff marks on the floor. It can also be used to clean your microwave and dishwasher.	Baking soda can be used for many purposes. It can be mixed with water to relieve insect bites. Do you have scuff marks on your floor? Use baking soda to get rid of them! The next time you clean your microwave and dishwasher, adding a little baking soda can help remove odors and stains.

WRITING STRATEGY

Minilesson 75

Introducing Sentence Fluency

Common Core State Standard: W.5.5

Objective: Understand how to use the information about sentence fluency that is presented in this lesson.

Guiding Question: How can I use these pages to help my sentences flow?

Teach/Model

Have students read page 88. Explain that the example on this page shows how a writer revised choppy sentences to turn them into fluent ones.

Practice/Apply

Have students read the examples on p. 89. Have them discuss how the examples show ways to make writing flow more smoothly.

Minilesson 76

Checking Sentences for Fluency

Common Core State Standard: W.5.5

Objective: Understand how to check sentences for fluency.

Guiding Question: How can I check the flow of my writing?

Teach/Model

Explain to students that the best way to check their own writing for sentence fluency is to read it aloud. Any choppiness or repetition will stand out to them when they hear how the sentences actually sound. Then they can make changes to help the sentences flow better.

Practice/Apply

Have students discuss how the student changed each piece of writing to improve sentence fluency. Have them read a sample of their own work, revising the writing for sentence fluency.

Conventions

Conventions

Conventions are rules for grammar, spelling, punctuation, and capitalization. When you edit your writing, you check for conventions.

Conventions

- Check your writing for errors in capitalization, grammar, punctuation, and spelling.
- Make sure you begin a new paragraph for each main idea. Remember to indent the first word of each paragraph.
- Use an editing checklist and check for common errors as you edit. Use editor's marks to show your changes.

Editing Checklist

Use an editing checklist to review your writing.

____ My sentences are of different lengths.

____ I have used different kinds of sentences.

____ My sentences are complete.

____ I have used punctuation correctly.

____ My words are all spelled correctly.

____ I have used capitalization correctly.

____ I have indented each paragraph.

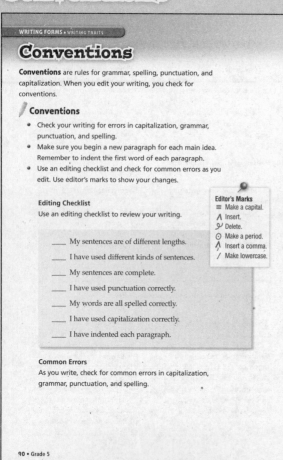

Editor's Marks
≡ Make a capital.
∧ Insert.
ℛ Delete.
⊙ Make a period.
∧ Insert a comma.
/ Make lowercase.

Common Errors

As you write, check for common errors in capitalization, grammar, punctuation, and spelling.

Irregular Verbs

An **irregular verb** is a verb that does not end with –ed in the past tense.

Wrong Way	Right Way
Last night, we gived our final performance.	Last night we gave our final performance.
The choir singed better than ever before.	The choir sang better than ever before.

Commonly Confused Words

Some words are easy to mix up. Make sure you're using the correct word.

Wrong Way	Right Way
Jonny and Daniel forgot they're coats at school, so there returning their to get them.	Jonny and Daniel forgot their coats at school, so they're returning there to get them.
Is this you're jacket?	Is this your jacket?
That bread tastes well.	That bread tastes good.

Verb Tense

Verb tense tells us what happened in the past, present, or future.

Wrong Way	Right Way
Last week I go for a dental appointment.	Last week I went for a dental appointment.
I saw Jonah next Thursday.	I will see Jonah next Thursday.

The Verb *Be*

Be is one of the most commonly misused verbs. It takes many forms.

Wrong Way	Right Way
I is going to Jamaica on vacation.	I am going to Jamaica on vacation.
We was going to the beach.	We were going to the beach.
Tina were excited about the trip.	Tina was excited about the trip.

WRITING STRATEGY

Minilesson 77

Introducing Conventions

Common Core State Standard: W.5.5

Objective: Understand how to use the information about conventions that is presented in this lesson.

Guiding Question: How can I use these pages to help me edit my writing for conventions?

Teach/Model

Have students read p. 90. Explain that the editing checklist on this page will help them correct convention errors they may have made.

Practice/Apply

Have students read the examples on p. 91. Have them discuss how the writer edited the example sentences for conventions.

Minilesson 78

Editing for Conventions

Common Core State Standard: W.5.5

Objective: Understand how to edit for conventions.

Guiding Question: How can I edit my writing for conventions?

Teach/Model

Explain to students that checking for conventions involves checking for grammar, capitalization, punctuation, sentence length, and spelling. Remind them to use editor's marks when correcting their drafts.

Practice/Apply

Ask students to practice editing for conventions on a draft of their own writing. Remind them to use editor's marks.

Writing Workshop

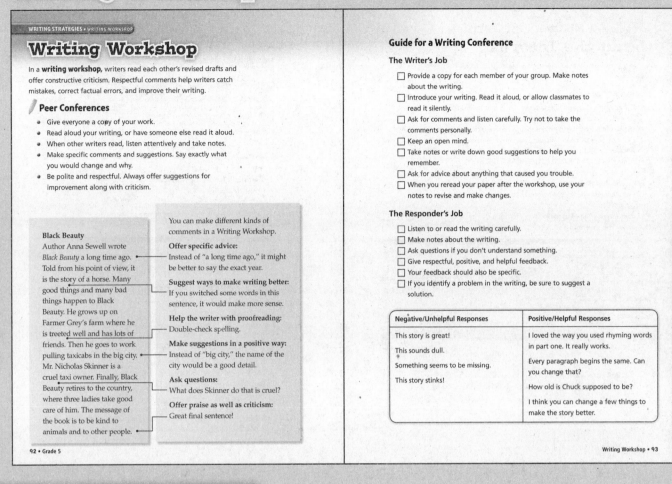

Writing Workshop

In a **writing workshop**, writers read each other's revised drafts and offer constructive criticism. Respectful comments help writers catch mistakes, correct factual errors, and improve their writing.

Peer Conferences

- Give everyone a copy of your work.
- Read aloud your writing, or have someone else read it aloud.
- When other writers read, listen attentively and take notes.
- Make specific comments and suggestions. Say exactly what you would change and why.
- Be polite and respectful. Always offer suggestions for improvement along with criticism.

Black Beauty

Author Anna Sewell wrote *Black Beauty* a long time ago. Told from his point of view, it is the story of a horse. Many good things and many bad things happen to Black Beauty. He grows up on Farmer Grey's farm where he is treeted well and has lots of friends. Then he goes to work pulling taxicabs in the big city. Mr. Nicholas Skinner is a cruel taxi owner. Finally, Black Beauty retires to the country, where three ladies take good care of him. The message of the book is to be kind to animals and to other people.

You can make different kinds of comments in a Writing Workshop.

Offer specific advice:
Instead of "a long time ago," it might be better to say the exact year.

Suggest ways to make writing better:
If you switched some words in this sentence, it would make more sense.

Help the writer with proofreading:
Double-check spelling.

Make suggestions in a positive way:
Instead of "big city," the name of the city would be a good detail.

Ask questions:
What does Skinner do that is cruel?

Offer praise as well as criticism:
Great final sentence!

Guide for a Writing Conference

The Writer's Job

- ☐ Provide a copy for each member of your group. Make notes about the writing.
- ☐ Introduce your writing. Read it aloud, or allow classmates to read it silently.
- ☐ Ask for comments and listen carefully. Try not to take the comments personally.
- ☐ Keep an open mind.
- ☐ Take notes or write down good suggestions to help you remember.
- ☐ Ask for advice about anything that caused you trouble.
- ☐ When you reread your paper after the workshop, use your notes to revise and make changes.

The Responder's Job

- ☐ Listen to or read the writing carefully.
- ☐ Make notes about the writing.
- ☐ Ask questions if you don't understand something.
- ☐ Give respectful, positive, and helpful feedback.
- ☐ Your feedback should also be specific.
- ☐ If you identify a problem in the writing, be sure to suggest a solution.

Negative/Unhelpful Responses	Positive/Helpful Responses
This story is great!	I loved the way you used rhyming words in part one. It really works.
This sounds dull.	
Something seems to be missing.	Every paragraph begins the same. Can you change that?
This story stinks!	How old is Chuck supposed to be?
	I think you can change a few things to make the story better.

Minilesson 79

Introducing the Writing Workshop

Common Core State Standard: W.5.5

Objective: Understand how to use the information about writing workshops that is presented in this lesson.

Guiding Question: How can I use these pages to help me get the most out of writing workshops?

Teach/Model

Have students read p. 92. Explain that the example on this page shows the kinds of comments a responder could make in a writing workshop.

Practice/Apply

Have students read the lists and examples on p. 93. Have them discuss what the writer and the responder should each do in a workshop. Point out the charts with negative and positive responses.

Minilesson 80

Holding a Workshop

Common Core State Standard: W.5.5

Objective: Understand the writer's role and the responder's role in a workshop.

Guiding Question: How can I improve my writing and help others in a workshop?

Teach/Model

Explain that, in a workshop, students should give and receive constructive criticism on each other's writing. This means that comments should be respectful and polite and should help writers improve their work.

Practice/Apply

Have students discuss what makes the negative responses unhelpful and what makes the positive ones helpful.

Using the Internet

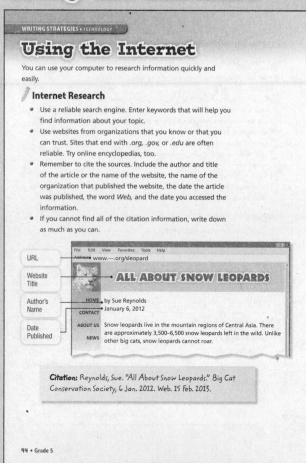

WRITING STRATEGY

Minilesson 81

Introducing "Using the Internet"

Common Core State Standard: W.5.6

Objective: Understand how to use the information about using the Internet that is presented in this lesson.

Guiding Question: How can I use these pages to help me do research on the Internet?

Teach/Model

Have students read through p. 95. Explain that the examples show the parts of a website page. Discuss the information about choosing a reliable source.

Practice/Apply

Have students discuss how to cite a source from a website, as well as how to avoid plagiarizing information from websites.

Minilesson 82

Using the Internet

Common Core State Standard: W.5.6

Objective: Understand how the Internet can be used for topic research.

Guiding Question: How do I use the Internet to help me research my topic?

Teach/Model

Explain that the Internet can provide useful information but that it is important to make sure sites are reliable. It also is important to cite sources and for writers to use their own words to relate the information.

Practice/Apply

Direct students to a reliable website. Together, practice citing a source and paraphrasing information from it.

Writing for the Web

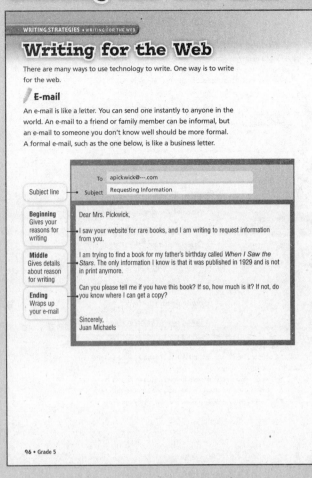

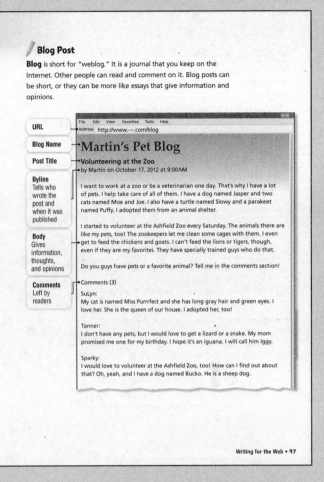

WRITING STRATEGY

Minilesson 83

Introducing "Writing for the Web"

Common Core State Standard: W.5.6

Objective: Understand how to use the information about writing for the web that is presented in this lesson.

Guiding Question: How can I use these pages to help me write for the web?

Teach/Model

Have students read pp. 96 and 97. Point out that e-mails are similar to letters, and blogs are similar to journals.

Practice/Apply

Have students discuss the organization of e-mails and blogs. Have them identify how the purpose of each type of writing for the web is reflected in its organization.

Minilesson 84

Writing E-mails and Blogs

Common Core State Standard: W.5.6

Objective: Understand how e-mails and blogs are written.

Guiding Question: How do I write e-mails and blogs?

Teach/Model

Explain that e-mails are like letters and that they can be either personal and informal or businesslike and formal. Explain that blogs give information and opinions in a journal format and that people can both read and comment on them.

Practice/Apply

With students, plan a class blog. Have them choose a blog name; then, have each student write an entry for the blog. Invite students to comment on others' entries.

Doing Research

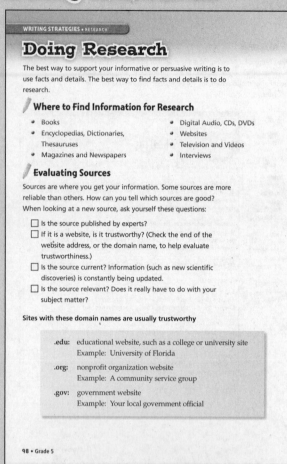

Doing Research

The best way to support your informative or persuasive writing is to use facts and details. The best way to find facts and details is to do research.

Where to Find Information for Research

- Books
- Encyclopedias, Dictionaries, Thesauruses
- Magazines and Newspapers
- Digital Audio, CDs, DVDs
- Websites
- Television and Videos
- Interviews

Evaluating Sources

Sources are where you get your information. Some sources are more reliable than others. How can you tell which sources are good? When looking at a new source, ask yourself these questions:

- ☐ Is the source published by experts?
- ☐ If it is a website, is it trustworthy? (Check the end of the website address, or the domain name, to help evaluate trustworthiness.)
- ☐ Is the source current? Information (such as new scientific discoveries) is constantly being updated.
- ☐ Is the source relevant? Does it really have to do with your subject matter?

Sites with these domain names are usually trustworthy

.edu:	educational website, such as a college or university site
	Example: University of Florida
.org:	nonprofit organization website
	Example: A community service group
.gov:	government website
	Example: Your local government official

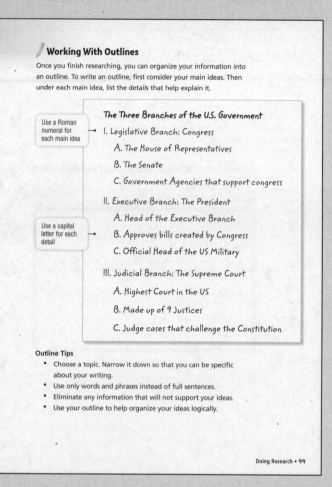

Working With Outlines

Once you finish researching, you can organize your information into an outline. To write an outline, first consider your main ideas. Then under each main idea, list the details that help explain it.

Use a Roman numeral for each main idea →

Use a capital letter for each detail →

The Three Branches of the U.S. Government

I. Legislative Branch: Congress
   A. The House of Representatives
   B. The Senate
   C. Government Agencies that support congress

II. Executive Branch: The President
   A. Head of the Executive Branch
   B. Approves bills created by Congress
   C. Official Head of the US Military

III. Judicial Branch: The Supreme Court
   A. Highest Court in the US
   B. Made up of 9 Justices
   C. Judge cases that challenge the Constitution

Outline Tips

- Choose a topic. Narrow it down so that you can be specific about your writing.
- Use only words and phrases instead of full sentences.
- Eliminate any information that will not support your ideas.
- Use your outline to help organize your ideas logically.

WRITING STRATEGY

Minilesson 85

Introducing Doing Research

Common Core State Standard: W.5.7

Objective: Understand how to use the information about research techniques that is presented in this lesson.

Guiding Question: How can I use these pages to help me do research?

Teach/Model

Have students read page 98. Explain that the list shows where to find information, as well as how to evaluate research sources for reliability.

Practice/Apply

Have students look at the example on p. 99. Explain that this example shows how to organize the results of research into an outline; it also gives tips on proper outlining.

Minilesson 86

Researching Reliable Sources

Common Core State Standard: W.5.7

Objective: Understand how to find reliable sources.

Guiding Question: How do I find reliable sources for my research?

Teach/Model

Explain that there are many different sources available to use for research on a topic. Note that it is important to check the sources for reliability and that writers must then organize the information they find.

Practice/Apply

Have students find other possible Internet sources for a research report on the U.S. Government. Have them explain how they know that each source is reliable.

Notetaking

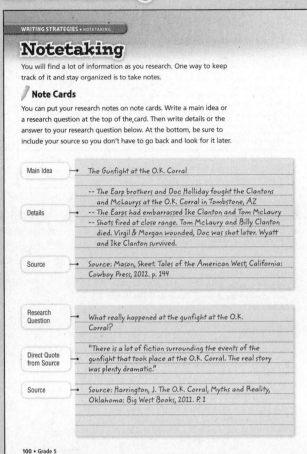

Notetaking

You will find a lot of information as you research. One way to keep track of it and stay organized is to take notes.

Note Cards

You can put your research notes on note cards. Write a main idea or a research question at the top of the card. Then write details or the answer to your research question below. At the bottom, be sure to include your source so you don't have to go back and look for it later.

Main Idea → The Gunfight at the O.K. Corral

Details →
-- The Earp brothers and Doc Holliday fought the Clantons and McLaurys at the O.K. Corral in Tombstone, AZ
-- The Earps had embarrassed Ike Clanton and Tom McLaury
-- Shots fired at close range. Tom McLaury and Billy Clanton died. Virgil & Morgan wounded, Doc was shot later. Wyatt and Ike Clanton survived.

Source → Source: Mason, Skeet. Tales of the American West, California: Cowboy Press, 2012. p. 144

Research Question → What really happened at the gunfight at the O.K. Corral?

Direct Quote from Source → "There is a lot of fiction surrounding the events of the gunfight that took place at the O.K. Corral. The real story was plenty dramatic."

Source → Source: Harrington, J. The O.K. Corral, Myths and Reality, Oklahoma: Big West Books, 2011. P. 1

100 • Grade 5

Another way to take notes for a research project is to make a grid. You can show information from more than one source.

Annie Oakley	Buffalo Bill's Wild West Show (book)	"Annie Oakley's Wild West" (magazine article)	"Annie Oakley" (Internet encyclopedia article)
Who was Annie Oakley?	exhibition shooter, performed with Buffalo Bill		born Phoebe Ann Mosley in Ohio in 1860; she began hunting at a young age
Why is she famous?	could do many tricks with a gun, toured around the US	most famous trick involved tossing a playing card in the air and shooting it	after she left the Wild West Show, she became an actress
Why did she join the Wild West Show?	started touring with circuses; joined Wild West Show with her husband Frank Butler		
What problems did she face?		many didn't take her seriously	poor family, didn't attend school
Why was she important?	first female superstar in America		set many shooting records
Other interesting facts	died in 1926 at age 66; Butler was so upset he stopped eating and died 18 days later	Famous quote: "Aim at a high mark and you shall hit it."	she also toured all over Europe

Notetaking • 101

Minilesson 87

Introducing Notetaking

Common Core State Standard: W.5.8

Objective: Understand how to use the information about notetaking that is presented in this lesson.

Guiding Question: How can I use these pages to help me take notes?

Teach/Model

Have students read p. 100. Explain that the note cards show how to organize research notes, with a main idea or research question at the top, and details, quotes, and sources that support it below.

Practice/Apply

Have students look at p. 101. Explain that the example on this page shows how to organize research notes into a note grid, with a column for each source.

Minilesson 88

Taking Notes

Common Core State Standard: W.5.8

Objective: Understand different methods of notetaking for research.

Guiding Question: How do I take organized research notes?

Teach/Model

Explain to students that there are different techniques used to take organized notes on a research topic. Writers can use a note card for each source, or they can put all of the sources and research on a note grid, which keeps all of the information together.

Practice/Apply

Give students source material from which to take notes. Have them choose one method of taking notes and explain why they chose this method.

Writing to a Prompt

Writing to a Prompt

Sometimes you are asked to do timed writing for class exercises and for tests in different subjects, like social studies and science. This is called writing or responding to a prompt.

Responding to a Prompt

- Read the entire prompt. Make sure to follow all the directions.
- Use your time carefully and work quickly.
- First, plan your writing. Jot down ideas and details as you think of them. You don't have to use complete sentences yet. Just use words and phrases to remind you what to write.
- Use your notes to write your response. At the end, if you have time, do a quick proofread of your writing.

Sample Prompt:

Two popular forms of energy are solar energy and oil.

Which do you think is the better source of energy? Why?

Write to convince a local senator to accept your point of view.

Notes:
Solar advantages
  -doesn't use resources
  -clean
Solar disadvantages
  -takes up lots of space
Oil advantages
  -affordable
  -have plenty now
Oil disadvantages
  -pollution
  -will run out
Solar better
  -won't run out
  -technology will improve

Response:
Solar power and oil each have advantages and disadvantages. Solar power is clean and doesn't use valuable resources. Oil is plentiful and affordable. But solar cells take up lots of room. Oil causes pollution and someday will run out.
In the long term, solar power is better because it won't run out as long as the sun shines. Solar cells will become smaller and more efficient in the future.

Types of Writing Prompts

There are different types of writing prompts that you may be asked to complete. Here are some of those types:

Narrative Prompt	Persuasive Prompt
Asks you to recount a personal or fictional experience or tell a story based on a real or imagined event	Asks you to convince the reader that your point of view is valid or that the reader should take a specific action
Informative Prompt	**Response to Literature**
Asks you to give information or explain why or how, to clarify a process, or to define a concept	Asks you to answer questions about something you read

Narrative Prompt:
Everyone has had a funny incident happen that they will never forget.
Think about a funny incident that has happened to you.
Now write a story describing this incident and how it happened.

Persuasive Writing Prompt:
Each U.S. president has had a unique impact on our country.
Which U.S. president do you think had the greatest effect?
Write an essay listing at least three reasons why you have chosen this president.

Informative Prompt:
Most people have at least one hobby.
Think about a hobby you have or know about.
Now write a description of your hobby and explain what materials you need.

Response to Literature Prompt:
Many people have a favorite poem or song that they like.
Think about a favorite poem or song that you like.
Now write to explain the meaning of this poem or song.

WRITING STRATEGY

Minilesson 89

Introducing "Writing to a Prompt"

Common Core State Standard: W.5.4

Objective: Understand how to use the information about writing to a prompt that is presented in this lesson.

Guiding Question: How can I use these pages to help me quickly and carefully respond to a prompt?

Teach/Model

Have students read p. 102. Explain that the sample response shows how to first take notes to support the main topic in a writing prompt and then to use those notes to write a response to the prompt.

Practice/Apply

Have students look at p. 103, which explains what various writing prompts ask writers to do. Discuss each type of prompt with students.

Minilesson 90

Responding to Different Kinds of Prompts

Common Core State Standard: W.5.4

Objective: Understand how to respond to different types of writing prompts.

Guiding Question: How do I write a quick but thorough response to a writing prompt?

Teach/Model

Explain that the best way to respond to any type of writing prompt is to start by making a plan or writing down ideas that support the topic. Then writers can use their notes to write their response, and, at the end, quickly review their writing for errors.

Practice/Apply

Have students choose one of the writing prompts and write a response to it.

Checklists and Rubrics

Checklists and Rubrics

Use this **rubric** to evaluate your writing. Circle a number in each
column to rate your writing. Then revise your writing to improve
your score.

Score	• Focus • Support	• Organization
Score **6**	**6** My writing is focused and supported by facts or details.	**6** My writing has a clear introduction and conclusion. Ideas are clearly organized.
Score **5**	**5** My writing is mostly focused and supported by facts or details.	**5** My writing has an introduction and a conclusion. Ideas are mostly organized.
Score **4**	**4** My writing is mostly focused and supported by some facts or details.	**4** My writing has an introduction and a conclusion. Most ideas are organized.
Score **3**	**3** Some of my writing is focused and supported by some facts or details.	**3** My writing has an introduction or a conclusion but might be missing one. Some ideas are organized.
Score **2**	**2** My writing is not focused and is supported by few facts or details.	**2** My writing might not have an introduction or a conclusion. Few ideas are organized.
Score **1**	**1** My writing is not focused or supported by facts or details.	**1** My writing is missing an introduction and a conclusion. Few or no ideas are organized.

• Word Choice • Voice	• Conventions • Sentence Fluency
6 Ideas are linked with words, phrases, and clauses. Words are specific. My voice connects with the reader in a unique way.	**6** My writing has no errors in spelling, grammar, capitalization, or punctuation. There are a variety of sentences.
5 Most ideas are linked with words, phrases, and clauses. Words are specific. My voice connects with the reader.	**5** My writing has few errors in spelling, grammar, capitalization, or punctuation. There is some variety of sentences.
4 Some ideas are linked with words, phrases, and clauses. Some words are specific. My voice connects with the reader.	**4** My writing has some errors in spelling, grammar, capitalization, or punctuation. There is some variety of sentences.
3 Some ideas are linked with words, phrases, or clauses. Few words are specific. My voice may connect with the reader.	**3** My writing has some errors in spelling, grammar, capitalization, or punctuation. There is little variety of sentences.
2 Ideas may be linked with words, phrases, or clauses. Few words are specific. My voice may connect with the reader.	**2** My writing has many errors in spelling, grammar, capitalization, or punctuation. There is little variety of sentences. Some sentences are incomplete.
1 Ideas may not be linked with words, phrases, or clauses. No words are specific. My voice does not connect with the reader.	**1** My writing has many errors in spelling, grammar, capitalization, or punctuation. There is no variety of sentences. Sentences are incomplete.

WRITING STRATEGY

Minilesson 91

Introducing the Rubric

Common Core State Standard: W.5.5

Objective: Understand how to use the information about
writing rubrics that is presented in this lesson.

Guiding Question: How can I use these pages to help me
understand rubrics?

Teach/Model

Have students look at the score column on p. 104.
Explain that the rubric scores go from 6 to 1 and that
students should strive to meet all the criteria to earn
a 6 in each category.

Practice/Apply

Have students look at the column headings on
pp. 104–105. Explain that the headings list the
writing traits their writing should achieve.

Minilesson 92

Evaluating Your Writing with a Rubric

Common Core State Standard: W.5.5

Objective: Understand how to self-evaluate writing.

Guiding Question: How do I use a rubric to evaluate my
writing?

Teach/Model

Explain to students that, in order to improve their
writing, they need to evaluate how well they
achieved the writing traits, such as focus, support,
organization, word choice, voice, conventions, and
sentence fluency. Model using the rubric to evaluate
a writing sample.

Practice/Apply

Have students evaluate their own writing against the
rubric, revising it to achieve the highest score.

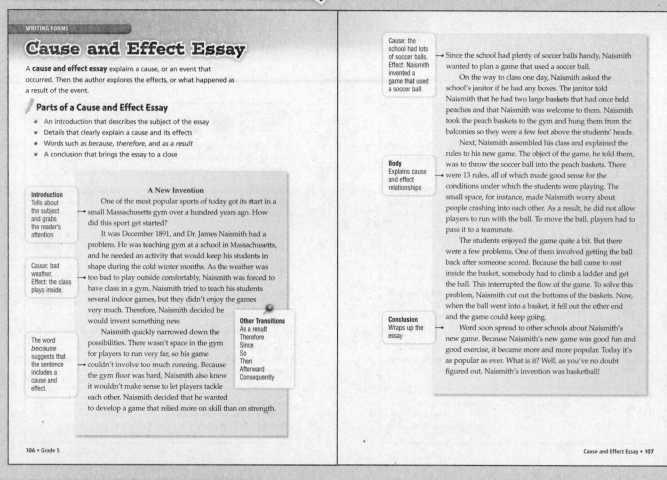

Cause and Effect Essay

Cause and Effect Essay

A **cause and effect essay** explains a cause, or an event that occurred. Then the author explores the effects, or what happened as a result of the event.

Parts of a Cause and Effect Essay

- An introduction that describes the subject of the essay
- Details that clearly explain a cause and its effects
- Words such as *because*, *therefore*, and *as a result*
- A conclusion that brings the essay to a close

Introduction
Tells about the subject and grabs the reader's attention

Cause: bad weather. Effect: the class plays inside.

The word *because* suggests that the sentence includes a cause and effect.

A New Invention

One of the most popular sports of today got its start in a small Massachusetts gym over a hundred years ago. How did this sport get started?

It was December 1891, and Dr. James Naismith had a problem. He was teaching gym at a school in Massachusetts, and he needed an activity that would keep his students in shape during the cold winter months. As the weather was too bad to play outside comfortably, Naismith was forced to have class in a gym. Naismith tried to teach his students several indoor games, but they didn't enjoy the games very much. Therefore, Naismith decided he would invent something new.

Naismith quickly narrowed down the possibilities. There wasn't space in the gym for players to run very far, so his game couldn't involve too much running. Because the gym floor was hard, Naismith also knew it wouldn't make sense to let players tackle each other. Naismith decided that he wanted to develop a game that relied more on skill than on strength.

Other Transitions
As a result
Therefore
Since
So
Then
Afterward
Consequently

Cause: the school had lots of soccer balls. Effect: Naismith invented a game that used a soccer ball.

Since the school had plenty of soccer balls handy, Naismith wanted to plan a game that used a soccer ball.

On the way to class one day, Naismith asked the school's janitor if he had any boxes. The janitor told Naismith that he had two large baskets that had once held peaches and that Naismith was welcome to them. Naismith took the peach baskets to the gym and hung them from the balconies so they were a few feet above the students' heads.

Body
Explains cause and effect relationships

Next, Naismith assembled his class and explained the rules to his new game. The object of the game, he told them, was to throw the soccer ball into the peach baskets. There were 13 rules, all of which made good sense for the conditions under which the students were playing. The small space, for instance, made Naismith worry about people crashing into each other. As a result, he did not allow players to run with the ball. To move the ball, players had to pass it to a teammate.

The students enjoyed the game quite a bit. But there were a few problems. One of them involved getting the ball back after someone scored. Because the ball came to rest inside the basket, somebody had to climb a ladder and get the ball. This interrupted the flow of the game. To solve this problem, Naismith cut out the bottoms of the baskets. Now, when the ball went into a basket, it fell out the other end and the game could keep going.

Conclusion
Wraps up the essay

Word soon spread to other schools about Naismith's new game. Because Naismith's new game was good fun and good exercise, it became more and more popular. Today it's as popular as ever. What is it? Well, as you've no doubt figured out, Naismith's invention was basketball!

WRITING MODELS AND FORMS

Minilesson 93

Understanding the Cause and Effect Essay

Common Core State Standard: W.5.2

Objective: Understand how to use the information about cause and effect essays that is presented in this lesson.

Guiding Question: How can I use these pages to help me write a good cause and effect essay?

Teach/Model

Have students read the definition and bulleted points. Add that the introduction should grab the reader's attention. Have students read through p. 107. Point out that the conclusion reviews the main points.

Practice/Apply

Have students find statements in the conclusion that restate ideas from the introduction.

Minilesson 94

Using Details to Show Effects

Common Core State Standard: W.5.2

Objective: Show the effects of an event.

Guiding Question: How do I use details to show what happened as the result of an event?

Teach/Model

Explain that the writer addressed one main idea in each paragraph and stated the effect at the start of the paragraph. The writer also used details to explore the effects and support the main ideas.

Practice/Apply

Have students circle the main idea of each body paragraph. Have them underline the details that support that main idea. Discuss the effects of the event stated in the introduction.

Problem-Solution Composition

WRITING FORMS

Problem-Solution Composition

A **problem-solution composition** describes a specific problem, or conflict, and then explores possible solutions to the problem.

Parts of a Problem-Solution Composition

- An opening paragraph that introduces the problem
- Specific examples to help define the problem
- A paragraph that explores possible solutions
- A conclusion to tie the ideas together

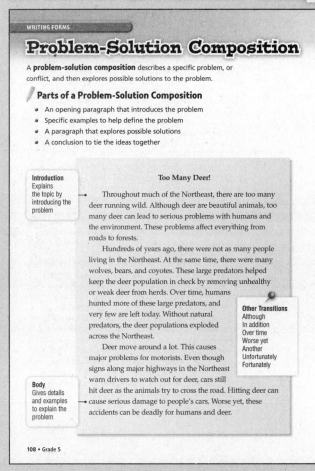

Introduction
Explains the topic by introducing the problem

Too Many Deer!

Throughout much of the Northeast, there are too many deer running wild. Although deer are beautiful animals, too many deer can lead to serious problems with humans and the environment. These problems affect everything from roads to forests.

Hundreds of years ago, there were not as many people living in the Northeast. At the same time, there were many wolves, bears, and coyotes. These large predators helped keep the deer population in check by removing unhealthy or weak deer from herds. Over time, humans hunted more of these large predators, and very few are left today. Without natural predators, the deer populations exploded across the Northeast.

Deer move around a lot. This causes major problems for motorists. Even though signs along major highways in the Northeast warn drivers to watch out for deer, cars still hit deer as the animals try to cross the road. Hitting deer can cause serious damage to people's cars. Worse yet, these accidents can be deadly for humans and deer.

Other Transitions
Although
In addition
Over time
Worse yet
Another
Unfortunately
Fortunately

Body
Gives details and examples to explain the problem

The author continues to expand on the problem by providing more examples.

Also, having too many deer can hurt forests and home gardens. Slow-growing trees like oak, ash, and maple grow all over the Northeast. Unfortunately, the leaves of young trees are a favorite food for deer. When deer enter a forest, they eat all the leaves before the young trees have a chance to grow big and strong. Without young trees replacing old ones, a forest will slowly die off.

Fortunately, there are many solutions to the deer problem. Mowing along roadways to cut down tall grass can reduce car crashes caused by deer. Drivers will be able to see deer before the animals wander into the road. This can save the lives of humans and deer. A possible solution to help save forests is to build tall fences around parts of the forests. These fences would keep out the deer. Then the young trees can keep growing and our forests can stay healthy. Everyone can help to put up these fences.

Solving the deer problem will take time. But it is worth it to make sure that animals and humans stay safe and happy.

Conclusion
Offers possible solutions and wraps up the essay

Note how the author of this essay:

- Began the essay by introducing the problem.

  Another way the author could have begun the essay is to paint a picture to grab the reader's attention.

  Sometimes it can be fun to see wild animals. Deer run fast and hide, so you don't often see them. Unfortunately, in some places, there are too many deer.

- Gave background information to explain the problem.

  Hundreds of years ago, there were not as many people living in the Northeast.

WRITING MODELS AND FORMS

Minilesson 95

Understanding the Problem-Solution Composition

Common Core State Standard: W.5.2

Objective: Understand how to use the information about problem-solution compositions that is presented in this lesson.

Guiding Question: How can I use these pages to help me write a good problem-solution composition?

Teach/Model

Have students read the definition and bulleted points. Have them read through p. 109. Point out that the conclusion suggests two solutions.

Practice/Apply

Have students circle the solutions in the conclusion and underline the details that support each solution.

Minilesson 96

Defining the Problem

Common Core State Standard: W.5.2

Objective: Explain a problem using details and examples.

Guiding Question: How do I use details and examples to explain a problem?

Teach/Model

Explain that the writer introduced the problem and then explained it using facts. Next, the writer expanded on the problems, giving supporting details for each.

Practice/Apply

Have students look for the topic introduced in the first paragraph. Then have them find the ideas in the following paragraphs that support and explain the topic.

Compare and Contrast Essay

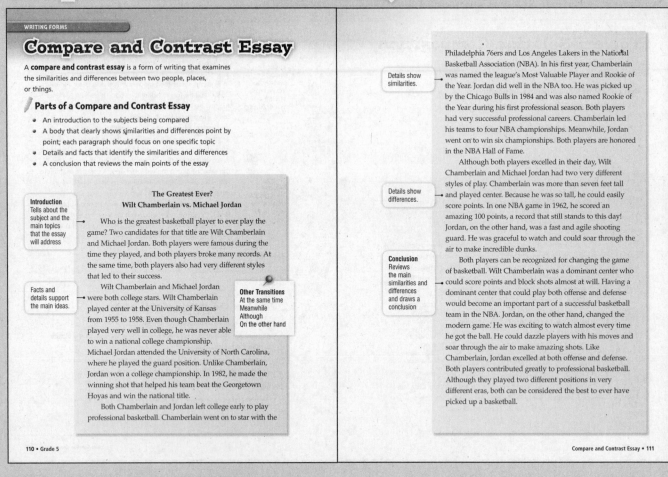

Minilesson 97

Understanding the Compare and Contrast Essay

Common Core State Standard: W.5.2

Objective: Understand how to use the information about compare and contrast essays that is presented in this lesson.

Guiding Question: How can I use these pages to help me write a good compare and contrast essay?

Teach/Model

Have students read the definition and bulleted points. Have students read through p. 111. Note that the essay shows both similarities and differences.

Practice/Apply

Have students make a Venn Diagram comparing and contrasting the subjects of the essay.

Minilesson 98

Organizing a Compare and Contrast Essay

Common Core State Standard: W.5.2

Objective: Show similarities and differences point by point.

Guiding Question: How do I keep my paragraphs focused?

Teach/Model

Explain that the writer introduced the similarities and differences between the subjects in the introduction. The writer then explained one similarity or difference, point by point, in each of the body paragraphs. Tell students that it is important to focus on only one main idea per paragraph.

Practice/Apply

Have students find the main idea for each body paragraph. Have them discuss how each paragraph's details relate only to the main idea.

How-to Essay

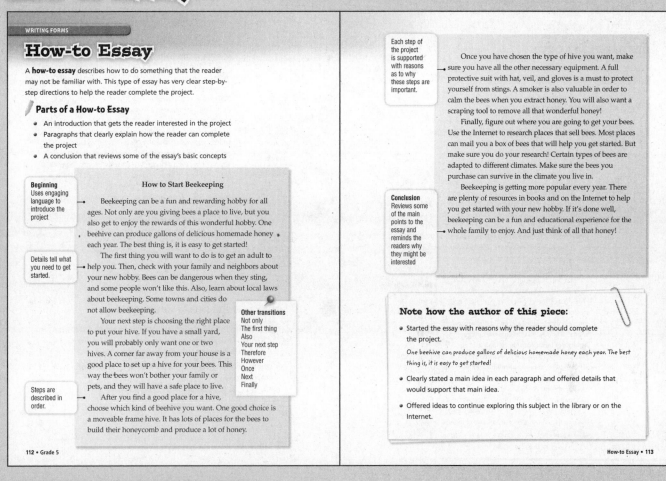

How-to Essay

A **how-to essay** describes how to do something that the reader may not be familiar with. This type of essay has very clear step-by-step directions to help the reader complete the project.

Parts of a How-to Essay

- An introduction that gets the reader interested in the project
- Paragraphs that clearly explain how the reader can complete the project
- A conclusion that reviews some of the essay's basic concepts

Beginning
Uses engaging language to introduce the project

Details tell what you need to get started.

Steps are described in order.

How to Start Beekeeping

Beekeeping can be a fun and rewarding hobby for all ages. Not only are you giving bees a place to live, but you also get to enjoy the rewards of this wonderful hobby. One beehive can produce gallons of delicious homemade honey each year. The best thing is, it is easy to get started!

The first thing you will want to do is to get an adult to help you. Then, check with your family and neighbors about your new hobby. Bees can be dangerous when they sting, and some people won't like this. Also, learn about local laws about beekeeping. Some towns and cities do not allow beekeeping.

Your next step is choosing the right place to put your hive. If you have a small yard, you will probably only want one or two hives. A corner far away from your house is a good place to set up a hive for your bees. This way the bees won't bother your family or pets, and they will have a safe place to live.

After you find a good place for a hive, choose which kind of beehive you want. One good choice is a moveable frame hive. It has lots of places for the bees to build their honeycomb and produce a lot of honey.

Other transitions
Not only
The first thing
Also
Your next step
Therefore
However
Once
Next
Finally

Each step of the project is supported with reasons as to why these steps are important.

Once you have chosen the type of hive you want, make sure you have all the other necessary equipment. A full protective suit with hat, veil, and gloves is a must to protect yourself from stings. A smoker is also valuable in order to calm the bees when you extract honey. You will also want a scraping tool to remove all that wonderful honey!

Finally, figure out where you are going to get your bees. Use the Internet to research places that sell bees. Most places can mail you a box of bees that will help you get started. But make sure you do your research! Certain types of bees are adapted to different climates. Make sure the bees you purchase can survive in the climate you live in.

Conclusion
Reviews some of the main points to the essay and reminds the readers why they might be interested

Beekeeping is getting more popular every year. There are plenty of resources in books and on the Internet to help you get started with your new hobby. If it's done well, beekeeping can be a fun and educational experience for the whole family to enjoy. And just think of all that honey!

Note how the author of this piece:

- Started the essay with reasons why the reader should complete the project.

  One beehive can produce gallons of delicious homemade honey each year. The best thing is, it is easy to get started!

- Clearly stated a main idea in each paragraph and offered details that would support that main idea.

- Offered ideas to continue exploring this subject in the library or on the Internet.

WRITING MODELS AND FORMS

Minilesson 99

Understanding the How-to Essay

Common Core State Standard: W.5.2

Objective: Understand how to use the information about how-to essays that is presented in this lesson.

Guiding Question: How can I use these pages to help me write a good how-to essay?

Teach/Model

Have students read the definition and bulleted points. Add that the essay should show what resources the reader needs to complete the project. Have the students read through p. 113. Point out that the transition words show the order in which the project's steps are done.

Practice/Apply

Have students underline the transition words and discuss how they keep the project's steps in order.

Minilesson 100

Writing Step-by-Step Instructions

Common Core State Standard: W.5.2

Objective: Explain the steps to complete a project, one step at a time, in order.

Guiding Question: How do I make sure the steps for my project are in order and are clear?

Teach/Model

Explain that the writer introduced the project and then explained how to do it, step by step. Each paragraph covers only one step of the project, and the paragraphs are in the order the reader must do the steps.

Practice/Apply

Have students underline the project step in each paragraph. Discuss how the details in each paragraph support only that paragraph's step.

Explanation

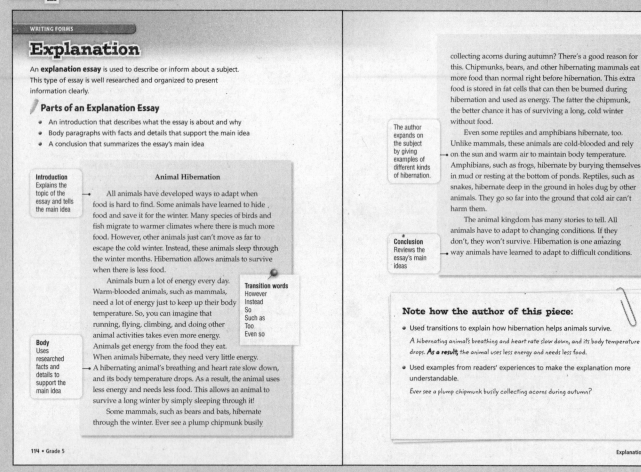

WRITING MODELS AND FORMS

Minilesson 101

Understanding the Explanation

Common Core State Standard: W.5.2

Objective: Understand how to use the information about explanation essays that is presented in this lesson.

Guiding Question: How can I use these pages to help me write a good explanation essay?

Teach/Model

Have students read the definition and bulleted points. Add that writers usually do research on the topic before writing an essay. Have students read through p. 115. Discuss how the writer connects with the reader's experience to explain the main idea.

Practice/Apply

Have students underline the main idea in the introduction and in the conclusion.

Minilesson 102

Supporting with Facts and Details

Common Core State Standard: W.5.2

Objective: Support the main idea with researched facts and details.

Guiding Question: How do I support the main idea with facts and details?

Teach/Model

Tell students that the writer explains the main idea by using facts and details. Emphasize that writers usually need to research the topic to find supporting information.

Practice/Apply

Have students choose a body paragraph and put its facts and supporting details into an idea-support map, ensuring that they understand how the writer supports the main idea.

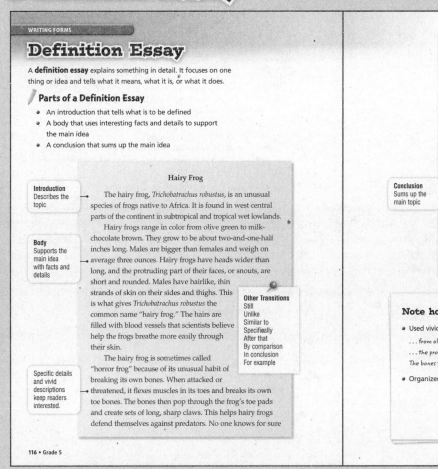

Definition Essay

WRITING FORMS

Definition Essay

A **definition essay** explains something in detail. It focuses on one thing or idea and tells what it means, what it is, or what it does.

Parts of a Definition Essay

- An introduction that tells what is to be defined
- A body that uses interesting facts and details to support the main idea
- A conclusion that sums up the main idea

Introduction
Describes the topic

Body
Supports the main idea with facts and details

Specific details and vivid descriptions keep readers interested.

Hairy Frog

The hairy frog, *Trichobatrachus robustus*, is an unusual species of frogs native to Africa. It is found in west central parts of the continent in subtropical and tropical wet lowlands.

Hairy frogs range in color from olive green to milk-chocolate brown. They grow to be about two-and-one-half inches long. Males are bigger than females and weigh on average three ounces. Hairy frogs have heads wider than long, and the protruding part of their faces, or snouts, are short and rounded. Males have hairlike, thin strands of skin on their sides and thighs. This is what gives *Trichobatrachus robustus* the common name "hairy frog." The hairs are filled with blood vessels that scientists believe help the frogs breathe more easily through their skin.

The hairy frog is sometimes called "horror frog" because of its unusual habit of breaking its own bones. When attacked or threatened, it flexes muscles in its toes and breaks its own toe bones. The bones then pop through the frog's toe pads and create sets of long, sharp claws. This helps hairy frogs defend themselves against predators. No one knows for sure

Other Transitions
Still
Unlike
Similar to
Specifically
After that
By comparison
In conclusion
For example

116 • Grade 5

what happens next, but some scientists think the bones might, sooner or later, pull back inside the skin and the wounds heal over.

Forests, rivers, and croplands make up the hairy frogs' natural habitat. They live mostly on land but return to water for breeding. Their eggs are laid on rocks in streams. Tadpoles are strong and have several rows of sharp teeth for help with eating.

Hairy frogs are meat-eaters. They feed on bugs, including grasshoppers, beetles, and spiders, and even slugs. Most likely, the worst enemy of the hairy frog is humankind. In Cameroon, hairy frogs are hunted for their meat, roasted, and eaten.

This species of frog, known for its strange bone-breaking habit, is a threatened species. As forests are cut down, hairy frogs are losing part of their natural habitat. But for now, hairy frogs are alive and well.

Conclusion
Sums up the main topic

Note how the author of this piece:

- Used vivid words and descriptions.
  - . . . from olive green to milk-chocolate brown.
  - . . . the protruding part of their faces, or snouts, are short and rounded.
  - The bones then pop through the frog's toe pads...
- Organized the information in a way that is clear and easy to understand.

Definition Essay • 117

WRITING MODELS AND FORMS

Minilesson 103

Understanding the Definition Essay

Common Core State Standard: W.5.2

Objective: Understand how to use the information about definition essays that is presented in this lesson.

Guiding Question: How can I use these pages to help me write a definition essay?

Teach/Model

Have students read the definition and bulleted points. Then have them read through p. 117. Note that the writer includes details that further describe facts. Point out that the writer concludes the essay with an important fact about the subject being defined.

Practice/Apply

Have students underline the main idea in the introduction and in the conclusion.

Minilesson 104

Writing Descriptive Definitions

Common Core State Standard: W.5.2

Objective: Describe the subject to be defined using vivid words.

Guiding Question: How do I keep readers interested in my definition of the subject?

Teach/Model

Tell students that the writer keeps readers interested in the subject by using specific facts and vivid descriptions. These descriptive details define the subject while bringing it to life.

Practice/Apply

Have students underline descriptive words and phrases that support facts and details about the subject. Ask them to write a paragraph that defines a different animal using descriptive details.

Writing for Common Core • **95**

Interview

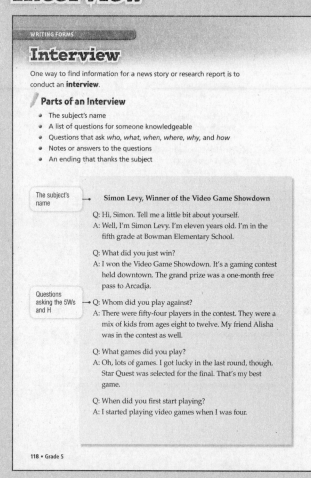

WRITING FORMS

Interview

One way to find information for a news story or research report is to conduct an **interview**.

Parts of an Interview

- The subject's name
- A list of questions for someone knowledgeable
- Questions that ask *who, what, when, where, why,* and *how*
- Notes or answers to the questions
- An ending that thanks the subject

The subject's name →

Simon Levy, Winner of the Video Game Showdown

Q: Hi, Simon. Tell me a little bit about yourself.
A: Well, I'm Simon Levy. I'm eleven years old. I'm in the fifth grade at Bowman Elementary School.

Q: What did you just win?
A: I won the Video Game Showdown. It's a gaming contest held downtown. The grand prize was a one-month free pass to Arcadia.

Questions asking the 5Ws and H →

Q: Whom did you play against?
A: There were fifty-four players in the contest. They were a mix of kids from ages eight to twelve. My friend Alisha was in the contest as well.

Q: What games did you play?
A: Oh, lots of games. I got lucky in the last round, though. Star Quest was selected for the final. That's my best game.

Q: When did you first start playing?
A: I started playing video games when I was four.

118 • Grade 5

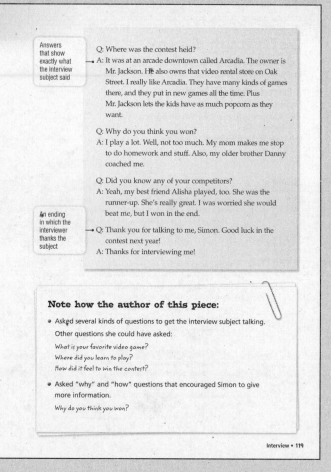

Answers that show exactly what the interview subject said →

Q: Where was the contest held?
A: It was at an arcade downtown called Arcadia. The owner is Mr. Jackson. He also owns that video rental store on Oak Street. I really like Arcadia. They have many kinds of games there, and they put in new games all the time. Plus Mr. Jackson lets the kids have as much popcorn as they want.

Q: Why do you think you won?
A: I play a lot. Well, not too much. My mom makes me stop to do homework and stuff. Also, my older brother Danny coached me.

Q: Did you know any of your competitors?
A: Yeah, my best friend Alisha played, too. She was the runner-up. She's really great. I was worried she would beat me, but I won in the end.

An ending in which the interviewer thanks the subject →

Q: Thank you for talking to me, Simon. Good luck in the contest next year!
A: Thanks for interviewing me!

Note how the author of this piece:

- Asked several kinds of questions to get the interview subject talking. Other questions she could have asked:
  What is your favorite video game?
  Where did you learn to play?
  How did it feel to win the contest?
- Asked "why" and "how" questions that encouraged Simon to give more information.
  Why do you think you won?

Interview • 119

WRITING MODELS AND FORMS

Minilesson 105

Understanding the Interview

Common Core State Standard: W.5.9

Objective: Understand how to use the information about interviews that is presented in this lesson.

Guiding Question: How can I use these pages to help me conduct an interview?

Teach/Model

Have students read through p. 119. Explain that the writer starts with general questions and then gets more specific. Point out that the writer concludes the interview by thanking the subject.

Practice/Apply

Discuss the information given in answers, and have students suggest follow-up questions that the writer could have asked Simon Levy.

Minilesson 106

Asking Good Questions

Common Core State Standard: W.5.9

Objective: Use a variety of questions to get the interview subject to talk.

Guiding Question: How do I get my interview subject to give me more information?

Teach/Model

Tell students that the writer gets the interview subject to talk more by asking a wide variety of questions. Note that *Why* and *How* questions encourage the interview subject to give more information.

Practice/Apply

Have students create five questions using *what, when, where, why,* and *how* to ask a classmate. Have them interview each other and write down their answers.

Business Letter/Science Observation Report

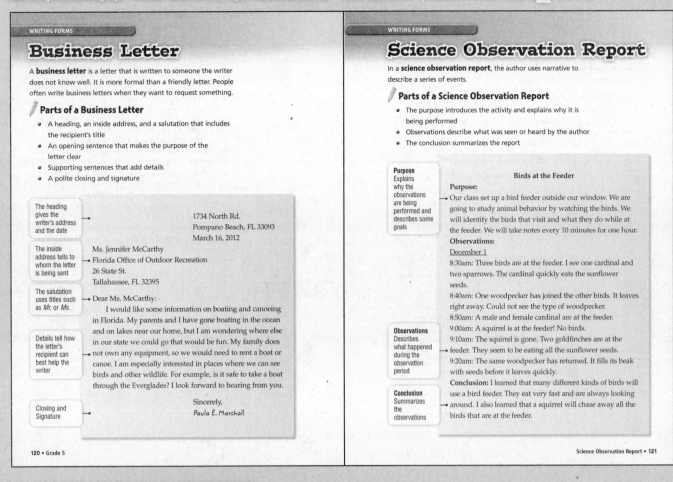

Minilesson 107

Understanding the Business Letter

Common Core State Standard: W.5.4

Objective: Understand how to use the information about business letters that is presented in this lesson.

Guiding Question: How can I use these pages to help me write a business letter?

Teach/Model

Have students read the definition and bulleted points. Point out differences between a business letter and a friendly letter. Have the students read the letter. Note that the writer addresses the recipient using titles such as *Mr.* or *Ms.*

Practice/Apply

Have students write a business letter requesting information. Remind them to use a formal tone.

Minilesson 108

Understanding the Observation Report

Common Core State Standard: W.5.8

Objective: Understand how to use the information about science observation reports that is presented in this lesson.

Guiding Question: How can I use these pages to help me write a report on my scientific observations?

Teach/Model

Have students read p. 121. Point out that observations are often put in chronological order. Note how the writer tells what was learned from the observations.

Practice/Apply

Have students brainstorm observation ideas and write goals and a plan for one idea.

Writing for Common Core • **97**

Research Report

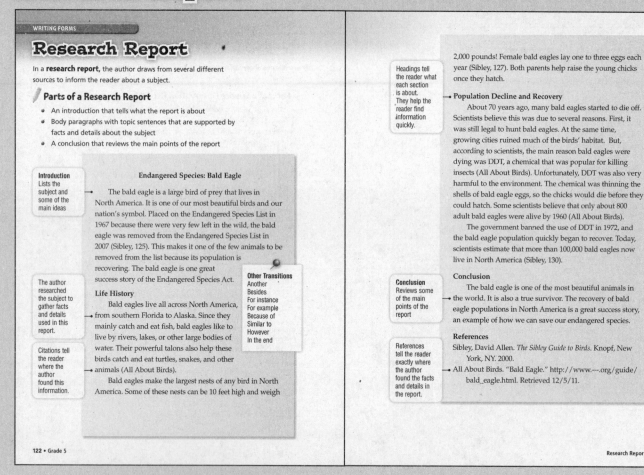

WRITING MODELS AND FORMS

Minilesson 109

Understanding the Research Report

Common Core State Standard: W.5.7

Objective: Understand how to use the information about research reports that is presented in this lesson.

Guiding Question: How can I use these pages to help me write a research report?

Teach/Model

Have students read and discuss the definition and bulleted points. Then have students read the report on pp. 122–123. Point out how the writer uses headings to help readers find information. Also note how the writer uses source citations in the text.

Practice/Apply

Have students highlight the citations in the report and match them with references at the end of the report.

Minilesson 110

Using Headings

Common Core State Standard: W.5.7

Objective: Use topic sentences and headings to present research in an organized report.

Guiding Question: How do I report my research in an organized way?

Teach/Model

Review the report on pp. 122–123, explaining how the writer uses an introduction, headings, topic sentences, and a conclusion to organize the research.

Practice/Apply

Have students take out the headings in the report. Then have them underline the topic sentences. Using the topic sentences as a guide, brainstorm alternate headings and write them on the report.

Graphs, Diagrams, and Charts

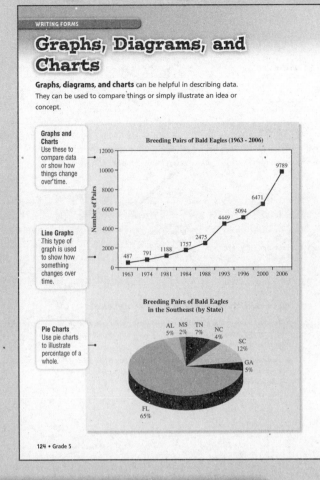

WRITING FORMS

Graphs, Diagrams, and Charts

Graphs, diagrams, and charts can be helpful in describing data. They can be used to compare things or simply illustrate an idea or concept.

Graphs and Charts
Use these to compare data or show how things change over time.

Line Graphs
This type of graph is used to show how something changes over time.

Pie Charts
Use pie charts to illustrate percentage of a whole.

Breeding Pairs of Bald Eagles (1963 - 2006)

Breeding Pairs of Bald Eagles in the Southeast (by State)

124 • Grade 5

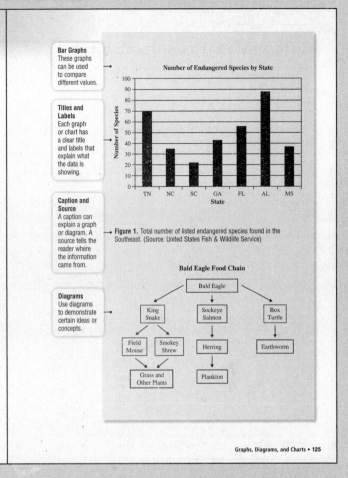

Bar Graphs
These graphs can be used to compare different values.

Titles and Labels
Each graph or chart has a clear title and labels that explain what the data is showing.

Caption and Source
A caption can explain a graph or diagram. A source tells the reader where the information came from.

Diagrams
Use diagrams to demonstrate certain ideas or concepts.

Number of Endangered Species by State

Figure 1. Total number of listed endangered species found in the Southeast. (Source: United States Fish & Wildlife Service)

Bald Eagle Food Chain

Graphs, Diagrams, and Charts • 125

WRITING MODELS AND FORMS

Minilesson 111

Understanding Graphs, Diagrams, and Charts

Common Core State Standard: W.5.8

Objective: Understand how to use the information about graphs, diagrams, and charts that is presented in this lesson.

Guiding Question: How can I use these pages to help me use graphs, diagrams, and charts to display data?

Teach/Model

Have students read pp. 124–125. Note that the graphs, diagrams, and charts have titles to tell readers what kind of data is displayed and that the bar graph has a caption and source.

Practice/Apply

Have students discuss how each graph, diagram, and chart is labeled to show particular types of data.

Minilesson 112

Choosing How to Display Data

Common Core State Standard: W.5.8

Objective: Choose a graph, chart, or diagram to describe data.

Guiding Question: What display should I choose to describe my data clearly?

Teach/Model

Tell students that the writer selected different types of graphs, diagrams, and charts depending on the type of data. For example, line graphs are often used to show how things change over time.

Practice/Apply

Have students brainstorm types of data they often see, such as plant height or student grades, and write them on the board. Ask students to choose an appropriate graph, chart, or diagram type for each type of data and explain their choice.

Multimedia Presentation

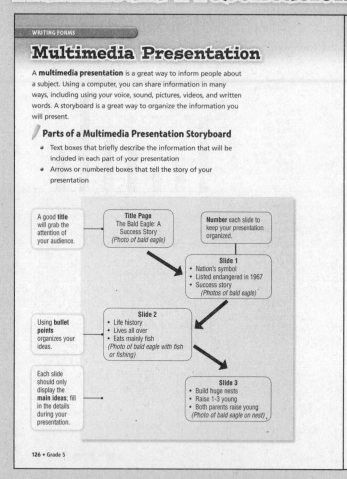
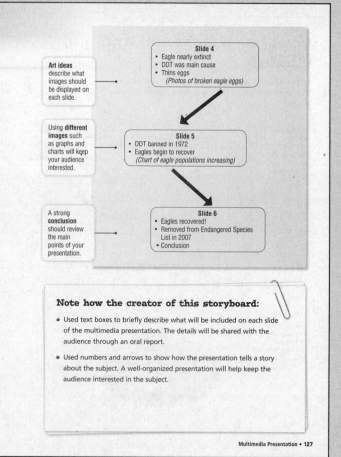

WRITING MODELS AND FORMS

Minilesson 113

Understanding the Multimedia Presentation

Common Core State Standard: W.5.6

Objective: Understand how to use the information about multimedia presentations presented in this lesson.

Guiding Question: How can I use these pages to help me create a multimedia presentation?

Teach/Model

Have students read pp. 126–127, discussing how the writer uses a storyboard to organize a slide presentation. Note that the text boxes are numbered.

Practice/Apply

Have students discuss other ways the writer could present the information, such as with video, sound, and pictures.

Minilesson 114

Creating a Storyboard

Common Core State Standard: W.5.6

Objective: Create a storyboard to organize information for a multimedia presentation.

Guiding Question: How do I use a storyboard to organize my presentation?

Teach/Model

Tell students that the writer used one slide per idea for the storyboard on pp. 126–127. Note how the text boxes describe the information each slide will include.

Practice/Apply

Give students copies of a storyboard without the slide numbers on the text boxes. Ask students to arrange the text boxes as a storyboard in the order they would present them.

Personal Narrative

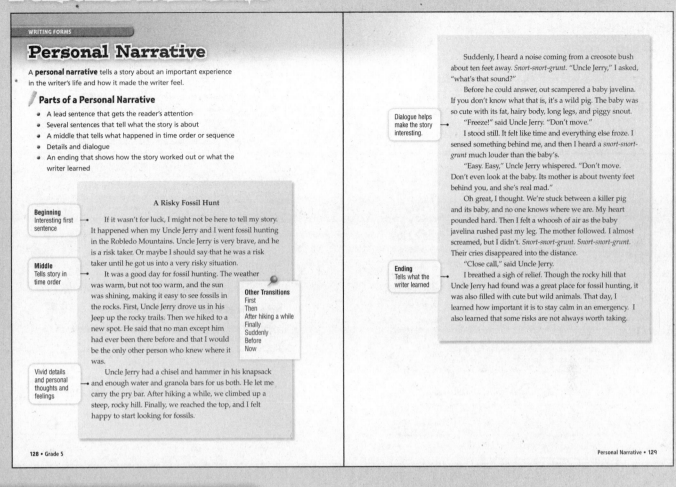

WRITING MODELS AND FORMS

Minilesson 115

Understanding the Personal Narrative

Common Core State Standard: W.5.3

Objective: Understand how to use the information about personal narrative presented in this lesson.

Guiding Question: How can I use these pages to help me write a personal narrative?

Teach/Model

Have students read the definition and bulleted points. Add that writers usually introduce the other characters at the beginning. Have students read pp. 128–129, discussing how the writer uses transition words to show the time sequence of events.

Practice/Apply

Have students underline the transition words, such as *suddenly* and *finally*, that show time sequence.

Minilesson 116

Using Details and Dialogue

Common Core State Standard: W.5.3

Objective: Use vivid details and dialogue to keep the reader interested in the story.

Guiding Question: How do I use details and dialogue to make my story interesting?

Teach/Model

Tell students that, rather than simply listing the events as they happened, the writer used vivid details and dialogue to make the story interesting.

Practice/Apply

Ask students to choose and underline a sentence in each paragraph that describes the scene, tells what the characters are saying, or describes the narrator's feelings. Discuss how the sentence enlivens the story.

Biography

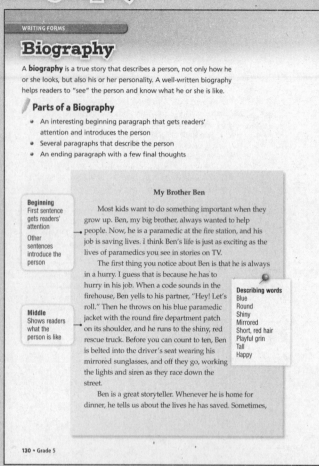

Minilesson 117

Understanding the Biography

Common Core State Standard: W.5.2

Objective: Understand how to use the information about biography that is presented in this lesson.

Guiding Question: How can I use these pages to help me write a biography?

Teach/Model

Have students read the definition and bulleted points. Add that writers often hold readers' interest by including details that give a clear picture of the subject of the biography. Have the students read pp. 130–131. Point out the beginning, middle, and ending.

Practice/Apply

Have students underline the details that describe the subject of the biography.

Minilesson 118

Showing and Not Telling

Common Core State Standard: W.5.2

Objective: Use details in a biography to show readers who the subject of the biography is and what he or she is like.

Guiding Question: How do I use details to show what kind of a person my subject is?

Teach/Model

Tell students that the writer used details about the subject to show readers what the person is like. The writer also used dialogue, which is another way to show readers the personality of the subject.

Practice/Apply

Ask students to choose a person they know and make a list of details that would show what that individual is like.

Fictional Narrative

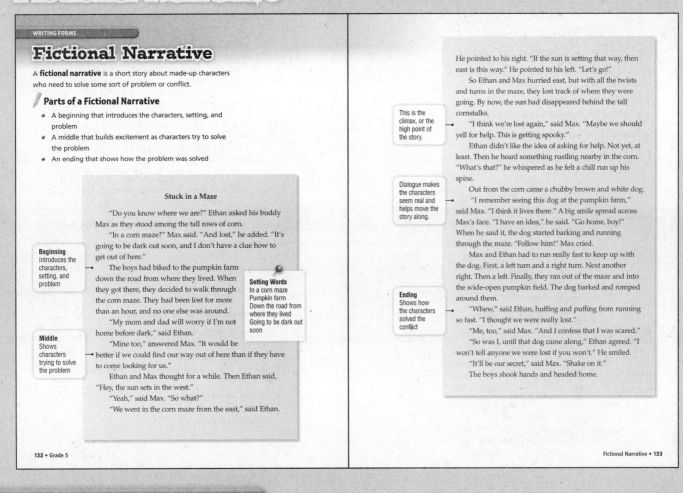

Fictional Narrative

A **fictional narrative** is a short story about made-up characters who need to solve some sort of problem or conflict.

Parts of a Fictional Narrative

- A beginning that introduces the characters, setting, and problem
- A middle that builds excitement as characters try to solve the problem
- An ending that shows how the problem was solved

Stuck in a Maze

"Do you know where we are?" Ethan asked his buddy Max as they stood among the tall rows of corn.

"In a corn maze?" Max said. "And lost," he added. "It's going to be dark out soon, and I don't have a clue how to get out of here."

Beginning Introduces the characters, setting, and problem

The boys had biked to the pumpkin farm down the road from where they lived. When they got there, they decided to walk through the corn maze. They had been lost for more than an hour, and no one else was around.

Setting Words In a corn maze / Pumpkin farm / Down the road from where they lived / Going to be dark out soon

"My mom and dad will worry if I'm not home before dark," said Ethan.

"Mine too," answered Max. "It would be better if we could find our way out of here than if they have to come looking for us."

Middle Shows characters trying to solve the problem

Ethan and Max thought for a while. Then Ethan said, "Hey, the sun sets in the west."

"Yeah," said Max. "So what?"

"We went in the corn maze from the east," said Ethan.

He pointed to his right. "If the sun is setting that way, then east is this way." He pointed to his left. "Let's go!"

So Ethan and Max hurried east, but with all the twists and turns in the maze, they lost track of where they were going. By now, the sun had disappeared behind the tall cornstalks.

This is the climax, or the high point of the story.

"I think we're lost again," said Max. "Maybe we should yell for help. This is getting spooky."

Ethan didn't like the idea of asking for help. Not yet, at least. Then he heard something rustling nearby in the corn. "What's that?" he whispered as he felt a chill run up his spine.

Out from the corn came a chubby brown and white dog.

Dialogue makes the characters seem real and helps move the story along.

"I remember seeing this dog at the pumpkin farm," said Max. "I think it lives there." A big smile spread across Max's face. "I have an idea," he said. "Go home, boy!" When he said it, the dog started barking and running through the maze. "Follow him!" Max cried.

Max and Ethan had to run really fast to keep up with the dog. First, a left turn and a right turn. Next another right. Then a left. Finally, they ran out of the maze and into the wide-open pumpkin field. The dog barked and romped around them.

Ending Shows how the characters solved the conflict

"Whew," said Ethan, huffing and puffing from running so fast. "I thought we were really lost."

"Me, too," said Max. "And I confess that I was scared."

"So was I, until that dog came along," Ethan agreed. "I won't tell anyone we were lost if you won't." He smiled.

"It'll be our secret," said Max. "Shake on it."

The boys shook hands and headed home.

Minilesson 119

Understanding the Fictional Narrative

Common Core State Standard: W.5.3

Objective: Understand how to use the information about fictional narrative that is presented in this lesson.

Guiding Question: How can I use these pages to help me write a fictional narrative?

Teach/Model

Have students read the definition and bulleted points. Then have students read pp. 132–133. Explain that the writer used vivid details to make the characters seem like real people and the setting seem like a real place.

Practice/Apply

Have students underline the vivid details and list other details that could be added to the narrative.

Minilesson 120

Solving the Problem

Common Core State Standard: W.5.3

Objective: Pose a problem and tell the story of how it was solved.

Guiding Question: How do I show how my characters solved a problem?

Teach/Model

Tell students that the writer posed a problem at the beginning of the story, built excitement to a climax, and then had the characters solve the problem at the end.

Practice/Apply

Ask students to brainstorm other possible solutions to end the story; write them on the board. Have students pick the most interesting solution from the list and write a new ending to the story.

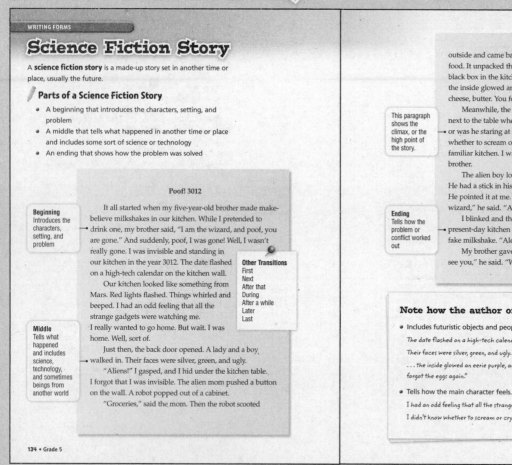

WRITING MODELS AND FORMS

Minilesson 121

Understanding the Science Fiction Story

Common Core State Standard: W.5.3

Objective: Understand how to use the information about science fiction presented in this lesson.

Guiding Question: How can I use these pages to help me write a science fiction story?

Teach/Model

Have students read pp. 134–135. Note that the story has a futuristic setting and aliens, both of which are common features of science fiction stories.

Practice/Apply

Have students underline elements of the story that relate to the future, space, or science and technology.

Minilesson 122

Putting the Science in Fiction

Common Core State Standard: W.5.3

Objective: Write a fictional story using science or technology as an important part of the story.

Guiding Question: How do I use science or technology in my story?

Teach/Model

Tell students that the story has a problem, just as any fictional narrative would, but that it includes details about the future and technology.

Practice/Apply

Ask students to think of an event that they experienced, such as a family vacation or a sporting event. Have them write the event as a story, adding scientific or technological details to make it a science fiction story.

Play

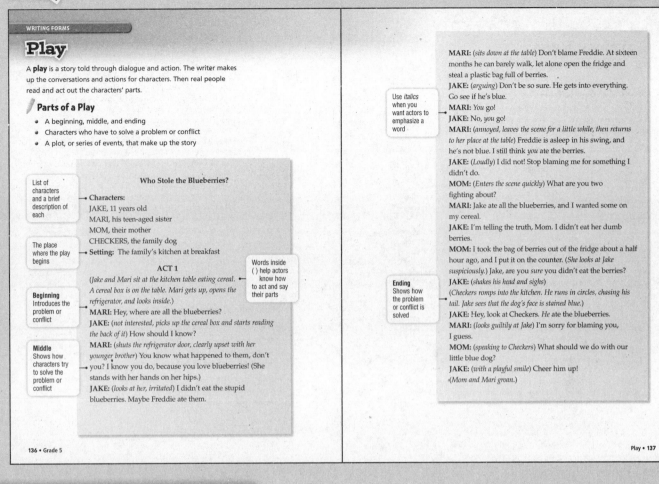

WRITING FORMS

Play

A **play** is a story told through dialogue and action. The writer makes up the conversations and actions for characters. Then real people read and act out the characters' parts.

Parts of a Play

- A beginning, middle, and ending
- Characters who have to solve a problem or conflict
- A plot, or series of events, that make up the story

List of characters and a brief description of each

The place where the play begins

Beginning Introduces the problem or conflict

Middle Shows how characters try to solve the problem or conflict

Who Stole the Blueberries?

Characters:
JAKE, 11 years old
MARI, his teen-aged sister
MOM, their mother
CHECKERS, the family dog
Setting: The family's kitchen at breakfast

ACT 1
(*Jake and Mari sit at the kitchen table eating cereal. A cereal box is on the table. Mari gets up, opens the refrigerator, and looks inside.*)
MARI: Hey, where are all the blueberries?
JAKE: (*not interested, picks up the cereal box and starts reading the back of it*) How should I know?
MARI: (*shuts the refrigerator door, clearly upset with her younger brother*) You know what happened to them, don't you? I know you do, because you love blueberries! (*She stands with her hands on her hips.*)
JAKE: (*looks at her, irritated*) I didn't eat the stupid blueberries. Maybe Freddie ate them.

Words inside ( ) help actors know how to act and say their parts

136 • Grade 5

Use *italics* when you want actors to emphasize a word

MARI: (*sits down at the table*) Don't blame Freddie. At sixteen months he can barely walk, let alone open the fridge and steal a plastic bag full of berries.
JAKE: (*arguing*) Don't be so sure. He gets into everything. Go see if he's blue.
MARI: You go!
JAKE: No, *you* go!
MARI: (*annoyed, leaves the scene for a little while, then returns to her place at the table*) Freddie is asleep in his swing, and he's not blue. I still think *you* ate the berries.
JAKE: (*Loudly*) I did not! Stop blaming me for something I didn't do.
MOM: (*Enters the scene quickly*) What are you two fighting about?
MARI: Jake ate all the blueberries, and I wanted some on my cereal.
JAKE: I'm telling the truth, Mom. I didn't eat her dumb berries.
MOM: I took the bag of berries out of the fridge about a half hour ago, and I put it on the counter. (*She looks at Jake suspiciously.*) Jake, are you *sure* you didn't eat the berries?
JAKE: (*shakes his head and sighs*)
(*Checkers romps into the kitchen. He runs in circles, chasing his tail. Jake sees that the dog's face is stained blue.*)
JAKE: Hey, look at Checkers. *He* ate the blueberries.
MARI: (*looks guiltily at Jake*) I'm sorry for blaming you, I guess.
MOM: (*speaking to Checkers*) What should we do with our little blue dog?
JAKE: (*with a playful smile*) Cheer him up!
(*Mom and Mari groan.*)

Ending Shows how the problem or conflict is solved

Play • 137

WRITING MODELS AND FORMS

Minilesson 123

Understanding the Play

Common Core State Standard: W.5.3

Objective: Understand how to use the information about plays that is presented in this lesson.

Guiding Question: How can I use these pages to help me write a play?

Teach/Model

Have students read the definition and bulleted points. Then ask them to read pp. 136–137. Note that the writer lists the characters and setting at the beginning and that the solution to the problem is presented through action and dialogue rather than description.

Practice/Apply

Have students underline the problem, the steps to the solution, and the solution to the problem.

Minilesson 124

Helping Your Actors

Common Core State Standard: W.5.3

Objective: Include directions for actors in a play.

Guiding Question: How do I help the actors know how to act and say their parts?

Teach/Model

Tell students that the writer uses dialogue and stage directions to pose a problem, tell a story about it, and show how the problem is solved. The stage directions, in parentheses, tell the actors how to act and say their lines.

Practice/Apply

Ask students to underline the stage directions in parentheses. Tell them to change a direction and explain how that affects how the actors say their lines.

Writing for Common Core • **105**

Opinion Essay

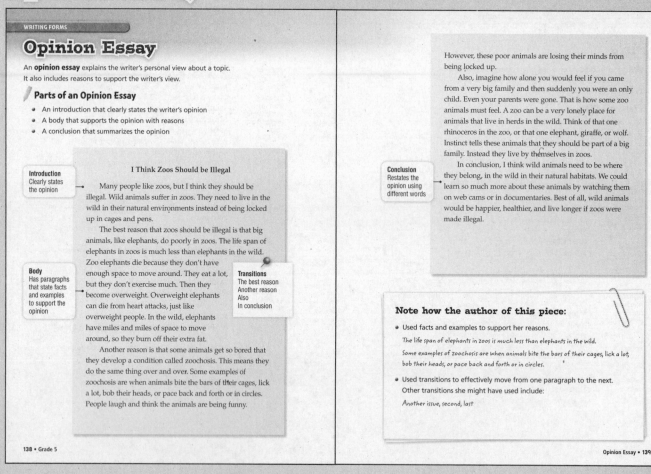

WRITING MODELS AND FORMS

Minilesson 125

Understanding the Opinion Essay

Common Core State Standard: W.5.1a

Objective: Understand how to use the information about opinion essays that is presented in this lesson.

Guiding Question: How can I use these pages to help me write a good opinion essay?

Teach/Model

Have students read the definition and bulleted points. Emphasize that an opinion essay should begin with a stated opinion. Explain that any opinion is valid as long as it is properly supported. Then have students read pp. 138–139.

Practice/Apply

Have students explain how the writer organized the reasons in her opinion essay (strongest reason first). Discuss other ways to organize the reasons.

Minilesson 126

Using Facts to Support an Opinion

Common Core State Standard: W.5.1b

Objective: Choose facts that will support my opinion.

Guiding Question: How do I choose facts that will support my opinion?

Teach/Model

Explain that the writer chose facts that are connected to the opinion. Tell students that the supporting facts in their essays should always be related to the main argument; those facts also should convince the reader to agree with the stated opinion.

Practice/Apply

Have students make a list of reasons and facts the writer gave to support the opinion. Remind them that facts can be proved, unlike opinions.

Persuasive Essay

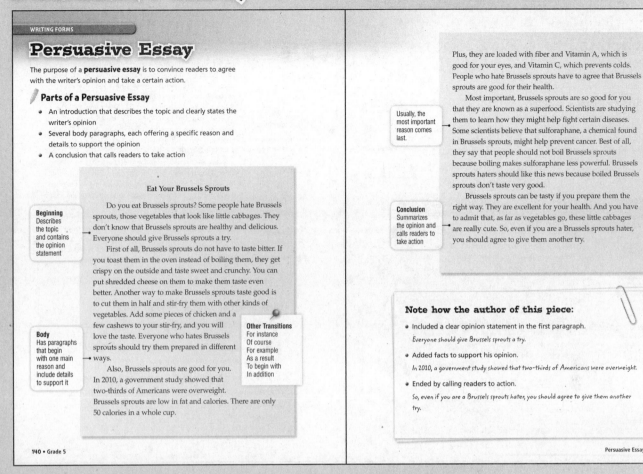

Persuasive Essay

WRITING FORMS

The purpose of a **persuasive essay** is to convince readers to agree with the writer's opinion and take a certain action.

Parts of a Persuasive Essay

- An introduction that describes the topic and clearly states the writer's opinion
- Several body paragraphs, each offering a specific reason and details to support the opinion
- A conclusion that calls readers to take action

Eat Your Brussels Sprouts

Beginning Describes the topic and contains the opinion statement

Do you eat Brussels sprouts? Some people hate Brussels sprouts, those vegetables that look like little cabbages. They don't know that Brussels sprouts are healthy and delicious. Everyone should give Brussels sprouts a try.

First of all, Brussels sprouts do not have to taste bitter. If you toast them in the oven instead of boiling them, they get crispy on the outside and taste sweet and crunchy. You can put shredded cheese on them to make them taste even better. Another way to make Brussels sprouts taste good is to cut them in half and stir-fry them with other kinds of vegetables. Add some pieces of chicken and a few cashews to your stir-fry, and you will love the taste. Everyone who hates Brussels sprouts should try them prepared in different ways.

Body Has paragraphs that begin with one main reason and include details to support it

Other Transitions
For instance
Of course
For example
As a result
To begin with
In addition

Also, Brussels sprouts are good for you. In 2010, a government study showed that two-thirds of Americans were overweight. Brussels sprouts are low in fat and calories. There are only 50 calories in a whole cup.

Plus, they are loaded with fiber and Vitamin A, which is good for your eyes, and Vitamin C, which prevents colds. People who hate Brussels sprouts have to agree that Brussels sprouts are good for their health.

Usually, the most important reason comes last.

Most important, Brussels sprouts are so good for you that they are known as a superfood. Scientists are studying them to learn how they might help fight certain diseases. Some scientists believe that sulforaphane, a chemical found in Brussels sprouts, might help prevent cancer. Best of all, they say that people should not boil Brussels sprouts because boiling makes sulforaphane less powerful. Brussels sprouts haters should like this news because boiled Brussels sprouts don't taste very good.

Conclusion Summarizes the opinion and calls readers to take action

Brussels sprouts can be tasty if you prepare them the right way. They are excellent for your health. And you have to admit that, as far as vegetables go, these little cabbages are really cute. So, even if you are a Brussels sprouts hater, you should agree to give them another try.

Note how the author of this piece:

- Included a clear opinion statement in the first paragraph.
  Everyone should give Brussels sprouts a try.
- Added facts to support his opinion.
  In 2010, a government study showed that two-thirds of Americans were overweight.
- Ended by calling readers to action.
  So, even if you are a Brussels sprouts hater, you should agree to give them another try.

140 • Grade 5

Persuasive Essay • 141

WRITING MODELS AND FORMS

Minilesson 127

Understanding the Persuasive Essay

Common Core State Standard: W.5.1d

Objective: Understand how to use the information about persuasive essays that is presented in this lesson.

Guiding Question: How can I use these pages to help me write a good persuasive essay?

Teach/Model

Have students read the definition and bulleted points on p. 140. Explain to students that the purpose of a persuasive essay is to convince the reader to agree with their opinion and take action.

Practice/Apply

Read pp. 140–141 with students. Have students identify the action the author wishes the reader to take.

Minilesson 128

Writing a Call to Action

Common Core State Standard: W.5.1d

Objective: Write a call to action.

Guiding Question: How do I write a convincing call to action?

Teach/Model

With students, review the concluding paragraph of the model on p. 141. Have students repeat in their own words what the writer wants readers to do. Remind students that the writer has provided reasons why the reader should accept the call to action.

Practice/Apply

Have students guide you to list topics for a persuasive essay on the board. Have them suggest a call to action to end each possible essay.

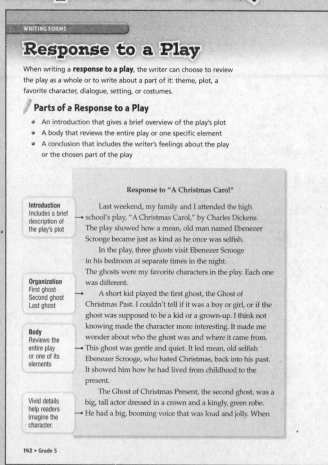

Minilesson 129

Understanding the Response to a Play

Common Core State Standard: W.5.9a

Objective: Understand how to use the information about a play response that is presented in this lesson.

Guiding Question: How can I use these pages to help me write a good response to a play?

Teach/Model

Have students read the definition and bulleted points. Explain that a response to a play should include the writer's thoughts and feelings about it.

Practice/Apply

Have students read pp. 142–143 and find the author's opinions about the play.

Minilesson 130

Writing a Review of a Play

Common Core State Standard: W.5.9a

Objective: Write a response that includes a brief overview of the play.

Guiding Question: How do I include a brief overview of the plot of the play in my response?

Teach/Model

Tell students that the beginning of their response should include a brief overview of the plot of the play.

Practice/Apply

Have students locate the overview of the plot in the model (on p. 142). Explain that this overview is brief, yet it gives readers an idea of what the play is about. Have students pick out the main plot points of the play as described in the model.

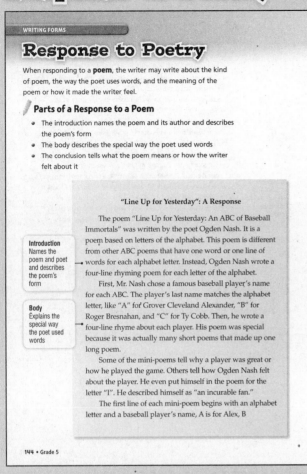

Response to Poetry

Response to Poetry

When responding to a **poem**, the writer may write about the kind of poem, the way the poet uses words, and the meaning of the poem or how it made the writer feel.

Parts of a Response to a Poem

- The introduction names the poem and its author and describes the poem's form
- The body describes the special way the poet used words
- The conclusion tells what the poem means or how the writer felt about it

"Line Up for Yesterday": A Response

Introduction
Names the poem and poet and describes the poem's form

The poem "Line Up for Yesterday: An ABC of Baseball Immortals" was written by the poet Ogden Nash. It is a poem based on letters of the alphabet. This poem is different from other ABC poems that have one word or one line of words for each alphabet letter. Instead, Ogden Nash wrote a four-line rhyming poem for each letter of the alphabet.

Body
Explains the special way the poet used words

First, Mr. Nash chose a famous baseball player's name for each ABC. The player's last name matches the alphabet letter, like "A" for Grover Cleveland Alexander, "B" for Roger Bresnahan, and "C" for Ty Cobb. Then, he wrote a four-line rhyme about each player. His poem was special because it was actually many short poems that made up one long poem.

Some of the mini-poems tell why a player was great or how he played the game. Others tell how Ogden Nash felt about the player. He even put himself in the poem for the letter "I". He described himself as "an incurable fan."

The first line of each mini-poem begins with an alphabet letter and a baseball player's name, A is for Alex, B

Each middle paragraph tells one thing about the poem and backs it up with facts, examples, or details.

is for Bresnahan, C is for Cobb. The second and fourth lines always end in a rhyme, like corn-born, love-glove, and truth-Ruth.

In just a few words, Mr. Nash shows what some of the players looked like. He describes things like Johnny Evers's jaw, a pitcher throwing to Roger Hornsby, and Mel Ott's restless right foot.

Conclusion
Tells how the writer felt about the poem, or what the poem means

As a baseball fan, I loved this poem by Ogden Nash. Some of his rhymes made me laugh. Many of them taught me things that I didn't know about these old-time baseball players. I especially liked how his words helped me to imagine these players in action.

Note how the author of this piece:

- Gave specific examples to explain how the poet uses words.
  The player's last name matches the alphabet letter, like "A" for Grover Cleveland Alexander, "B" for Roger Bresnahan, and "C" for Ty Cobb.
- Ended the response by telling how he feels about Ogden Nash's poem. Other ways he could have ended the response are to tell what he thinks the poem means, or explain why he thinks Ogden Nash wrote it:
  Ogden Nash's poem means that baseball has had many great players.
  I think Ogden Nash wrote this poem because he really loved baseball.

WRITING MODELS AND FORMS

Minilesson 131

Understanding the Response to Poetry

Common Core State Standard: W.5.9a

Objective: Understand how to use the information about a poetry response that is presented in this lesson.

Guiding Question: How can I use these pages to help me write a good response to poetry?

Teach/Model

Have students read the definition and bulleted points. Emphasize that a response to poetry can focus on one element of the poem or the entire poem.

Practice/Apply

Read pp. 144–145 with students, discussing which elements of the poem the writer focused on.

Minilesson 132

Using Examples from the Poem

Common Core State Standard: W.5.9a

Objective: Use examples from the poem in a response.

Guiding Question: How do I use examples from the poem in my response?

Teach/Model

Explain to students that the writer of the model used examples from the poem to describe why the poem was special.

Practice/Apply

Have students locate the examples used by the writer of the model. Discuss how the examples gave the reader a feeling for what the poem was about. Ask students for their opinions of the poem based on this writer's response.

Author Response

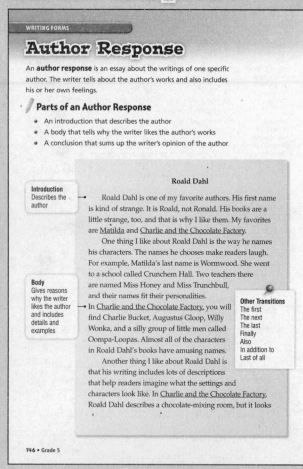

WRITING FORMS

Author Response

An **author response** is an essay about the writings of one specific author. The writer tells about the author's works and also includes his or her own feelings.

Parts of an Author Response
- An introduction that describes the author
- A body that tells why the writer likes the author's works
- A conclusion that sums up the writer's opinion of the author

Introduction
Describes the author

Roald Dahl

Roald Dahl is one of my favorite authors. His first name is kind of strange. It is Roald, not Ronald. His books are a little strange, too, and that is why I like them. My favorites are Matilda and Charlie and the Chocolate Factory.

One thing I like about Roald Dahl is the way he names his characters. The names he chooses make readers laugh. For example, Matilda's last name is Wormwood. She went to a school called Crunchem Hall. Two teachers there are named Miss Honey and Miss Trunchbull, and their names fit their personalities.

Body
Gives reasons why the writer likes the author and includes details and examples

In Charlie and the Chocolate Factory, you will find Charlie Bucket, Augustus Gloop, Willy Wonka, and a silly group of little men called Oompa-Loopas. Almost all of the characters in Roald Dahl's books have amusing names.

Another thing I like about Roald Dahl is that his writing includes lots of descriptions that help readers imagine what the settings and characters look like. In Charlie and the Chocolate Factory, Roald Dahl describes a chocolate-mixing room, but it looks

Other Transitions
The first
The next
The last
Finally
Also
In addition to
Last of all

146 • Grade 5

like a garden. Everything there is made of candy, and he even put a chocolate lake into the scene. In Matilda, he makes Matilda's super powers believable. You can imagine her staring hard at a glass of water and making it tip over or making a piece of chalk write on the blackboard just by looking at it.

My favorite thing about Roald Dahl's writing is that it can be scary. Some kids don't like his books because of that, but I do. You never know what is going to happen. Maybe an ordinary thing will become weird, like a peach growing as big as a house. A giant might show up and poke his finger through the window, or maybe a shark will come out of nowhere and attack. You never know with Roald Dahl.

Conclusion
Sums up the writer's feelings about the author

Roald Dahl died a while ago. I wish that he were still here to write more stories, but I will never get tired of his books. Some of them I have read more than once. In my opinion, Roald Dahl is one of the greatest authors who ever lived.

Note how the writer of this piece:
- Included several strong reasons why he likes this author.

  One thing I like about Roald Dahl is the way he names his characters.

  Another thing I like about Roald Dahl is that his writing includes lots of descriptions ...

  My favorite thing about Roald Dahl's writing is that it can be scary.

- Organized his reasons, putting the most important one last.

Author Response • 147

WRITING MODELS AND FORMS

Minilesson 133

Understanding the Author Response

Common Core State Standard: W.5.9a

Objective: Understand how to use the information about the author response that is presented in these pages.

Guiding Question: How can I use these pages to help me write a good author response?

Teach/Model

Have students read the definition and bulleted points. Explain that, for an author response, a writer can write about several texts by an author.

Practice/Apply

Have students read pp.146–147. Discuss how the writer uses examples from several texts to illustrate the main points.

Minilesson 134

Organizing Details

Common Core State Standard: W.5.4

Objective: Organize details in an author response.

Guiding Question: How do I organize my details in an author response to have the most impact?

Teach/Model

Explain that the writer of the response listed several reasons for liking this author. Point out that the details are listed in a logical order.

Practice/Apply

Ask students why the author put the most important detail last. Have students make a list of reasons they enjoy reading books by their favorite author. Have them arrange their reasons in a logical order.

Book Review

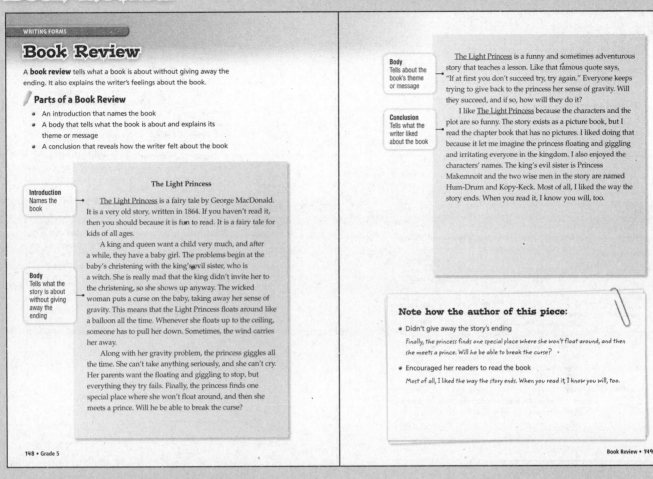

WRITING FORMS

Book Review

A **book review** tells what a book is about without giving away the ending. It also explains the writer's feelings about the book.

Parts of a Book Review

- An introduction that names the book
- A body that tells what the book is about and explains its theme or message
- A conclusion that reveals how the writer felt about the book

Introduction
Names the book

The Light Princess

The Light Princess is a fairy tale by George MacDonald. It is a very old story, written in 1864. If you haven't read it, then you should because it is fun to read. It is a fairy tale for kids of all ages.

Body
Tells what the story is about without giving away the ending

A king and queen want a child very much, and after a while, they have a baby girl. The problems begin at the baby's christening with the king's evil sister, who is a witch. She is really mad that the king didn't invite her to the christening, so she shows up anyway. The wicked woman puts a curse on the baby, taking away her sense of gravity. This means that the Light Princess floats around like a balloon all the time. Whenever she floats up to the ceiling, someone has to pull her down. Sometimes, the wind carries her away.

Along with her gravity problem, the princess giggles all the time. She can't take anything seriously, and she can't cry. Her parents want the floating and giggling to stop, but everything they try fails. Finally, the princess finds one special place where she won't float around, and then she meets a prince. Will he be able to break the curse?

148 • Grade 5

Body
Tells about the book's theme or message

The Light Princess is a funny and sometimes adventurous story that teaches a lesson. Like that famous quote says, "If at first you don't succeed try, try again." Everyone keeps trying to give back to the princess her sense of gravity. Will they succeed, and if so, how will they do it?

Conclusion
Tells what the writer liked about the book

I like The Light Princess because the characters and the plot are so funny. The story exists as a picture book, but I read the chapter book that has no pictures. I liked doing that because it let me imagine the princess floating and giggling and irritating everyone in the kingdom. I also enjoyed the characters' names. The king's evil sister is Princess Makemnoit and the two wise men in the story are named Hum-Drum and Kopy-Keck. Most of all, I liked the way the story ends. When you read it, I know you will, too.

Note how the author of this piece:

- Didn't give away the story's ending

  Finally, the princess finds one special place where she won't float around, and then she meets a prince. Will he be able to break the curse?

- Encouraged her readers to read the book

  Most of all, I liked the way the story ends. When you read it, I know you will, too.

Book Review • 149

WRITING MODELS AND FORMS

Minilesson 135

Understanding the Book Review

Common Core State Standard: W.5.9a

Objective: Understand how to use the information about book reviews presented in this lesson.

Guiding Question: How can I use these pages to help me write a good book review?

Teach/Model

Have students read the definition and bulleted points and the rest of pp. 148–149. Point out how the review includes a summary that does not reveal the ending.

Practice/Apply

Discuss the book review, asking students how the author felt about the book. Have them cite examples from the review to support their views.

Minilesson 136

Using Transitions

Common Core State Standard: W.5.2c

Objective: Use a variety of transitions to write a book review.

Guiding Question: How do I use transitional words and phrases to write a book review?

Teach/Model

Explain to students that a book review includes a summary of the plot of the book. Point out the transitions that show time order, such as *after a while* and *finally*.

Practice/Apply

Have students point out the transitions the writer used in the summary. Ask students to suggest other transition words and phrases that could be used instead.

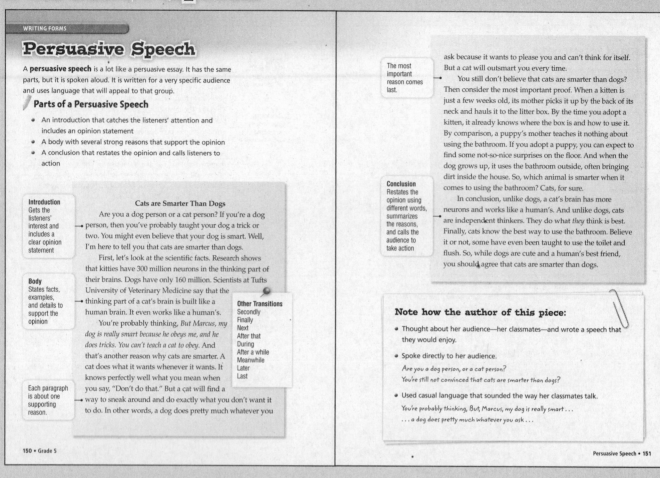

Minilesson 137

Understanding the Persuasive Speech

Common Core State Standard: W.5.1a

Objective: Understand how to use the information about a persuasive speech that is presented in this lesson.

Guiding Question: How can I use these pages to help me write a good persuasive speech?

Teach/Model

Have students read pp. 150–151. Emphasize that a speech is written to be spoken in front of an audience that the speaker should address directly.

Practice/Apply

Ask a volunteer to read the model aloud. Ask students to give examples from the speech that show how the writer used language appropriate for this audience.

Minilesson 138

Writing a Strong Conclusion

Common Core State Standard: W.5.1d

Objective: Write a strong conclusion for a persuasive speech.

Guiding Question: How do I write a strong conclusion for a persuasive speech?

Teach/Model

Explain that a persuasive speech should have a strong conclusion that restates the opinion and includes a call to action. Have a volunteer reread the conclusion in the model.

Practice/Apply

Ask students to identify the author's restated opinion and the call to action. Have students rewrite a conclusion for this speech. Ask for volunteers to share their new conclusion with the class.

Labels and Captions

WRITING FORMS

Labels and Captions

A **label** explains what a picture is, and a **caption** adds information to a picture. A label uses one or several words. A caption includes one or more complete sentences.

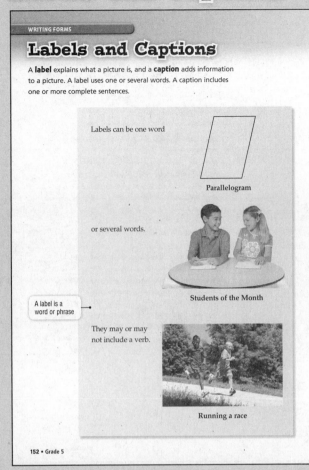

Labels can be one word

Parallelogram

or several words.

Students of the Month

A label is a word or phrase

They may or may not include a verb.

Running a race

152 • Grade 5

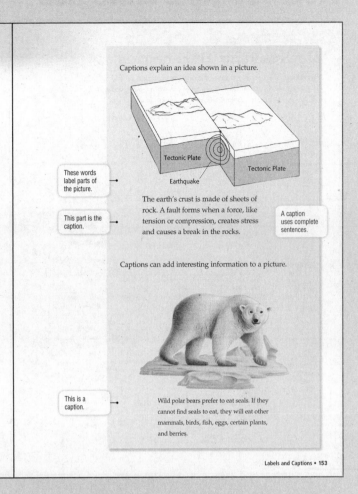

Captions explain an idea shown in a picture.

Tectonic Plate

Tectonic Plate

Earthquake

These words label parts of the picture.

This part is the caption.

The earth's crust is made of sheets of rock. A fault forms when a force, like tension or compression, creates stress and causes a break in the rocks.

A caption uses complete sentences.

Captions can add interesting information to a picture.

This is a caption.

Wild polar bears prefer to eat seals. If they cannot find seals to eat, they will eat other mammals, birds, fish, eggs, certain plants, and berries.

Labels and Captions • 153

WRITING MODELS AND FORMS

Minilesson 139

Understanding Labels and Captions

Common Core State Standard: W.5.8

Objective: Understand how to use the information about labels and captions that is presented in this lesson.

Guiding Question: How can I use these pages to help me write labels and captions?

Teach/Model

Have students read the definition and discuss the models on pp. 152–153. Explain the differences between labels and captions.

Practice/Apply

Show students examples of labels and captions in magazines and textbooks. Discuss how to determine when to use each.

Minilesson 140

Writing Labels and Captions

Common Core State Standard: W.5.8

Objective: Write labels and captions.

Guiding Question: How do I write effective labels and captions?

Teach/Model

Explain to students that they can use labels or captions to help readers understand photos, illustrations, and charts.

Practice/Apply

Show students photos from a magazine. Have students write a label and a caption for each photo. Go over students' work as a group.

Notetaking Strategies

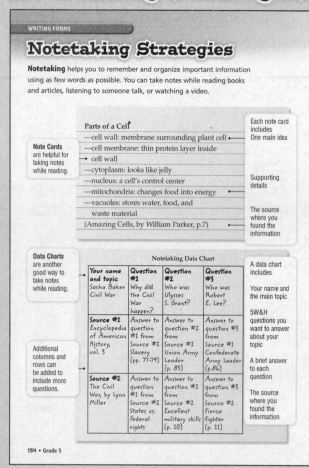

Notetaking Strategies

Notetaking helps you to remember and organize important information using as few words as possible. You can take notes while reading books and articles, listening to someone talk, or watching a video.

Note Cards are helpful for taking notes while reading.

Parts of a Cell
—cell wall: membrane surrounding plant cell
—cell membrane: thin protein layer inside
• cell wall
—cytoplasm: looks like jelly
—nucleus: a cell's control center
—mitochondria: changes food into energy
—vacuoles: stores water, food, and
    waste material
(Amazing Cells, by William Parker, p.7)

Each note card includes
One main idea

Supporting details

The source where you found the information

Data Charts are another good way to take notes while reading.

Additional columns and rows can be added to include more questions.

Notetaking Data Chart

Your name and topic Sasha Baker Civil War	Question #1 Why did the Civil War happen?	Question #2 Who was Ulysses S. Grant?	Question #3 Who was Robert E. Lee?
Source #1 Encyclopedia of American History, vol. 3	Answer to question #1 from Source #1 Slavery (pp. 77-79)	Answer to question #2 from Source #1 Union Army Leader (p. 85)	Answer to question #3 from Source #1 Confederate Army Leader (p.86)
Source #2 The Civil War, by Lynn Miller	Answer to question #1 from Source #2 States vs. Federal rights	Answer to question #2 from Source #2 Excellent military skills (p. 10)	Answer to question #3 from Source #2 Fierce fighter (p. 11)

A data chart includes

Your name and the main topic

5W&H questions you want to answer about your topic

A brief answer to each question

The source where you found the information

Good notetaking requires practice. When reading and listening, make sure that you understand the information so your notes will be correct. When listening, stay focused so you hear everything the speaker says. The more you practice notetaking, the easier it will become.

Build Your Notetaking Skills

- Pay attention to what you read, hear, or see.
- When listening, write quickly but neatly enough so you can read it later.
- Write down only what is necessary: main ideas and important details. No need to make full sentences.
- Use your own words. Don't copy information word-for-word from articles and books unless you plan to cite the words as a quote in your writing.
- Summarize big pieces of information.
- Draw pictures if they will help you to remember something.
- Organize your information clearly using numbers or transitions like *first, second, third*.
- Be accurate when writing down your sources. Use the title, author's name, and the page number(s) where you found the information.
- Read over your notes right away. Fix anything that is unclear or hard to read.
- Put a star next to main ideas, or highlight them with a marker.

WRITING MODELS AND FORMS

Minilesson 141

Understanding Notetaking Strategies

Common Core State Standard: W.5.8

Objective: Understand how to use the information about notetaking strategies that is presented in this lesson.

Guiding Question: How can I use these pages to help me take good notes?

Teach/Model

Have students read the definition. Discuss how good notes will save them time when studying or writing and also help them determine what information is important.

Practice/Apply

Read and discuss pp. 154–155. Practice creating a note card with notes about a historical figure you have studied.

Minilesson 142

Taking Notes While Listening

Common Core State Standard: W.5.8

Objective: Take notes while listening.

Guiding Question: How do I take notes while listening to a speaker?

Teach/Model

Explain to students that they can become better learners by taking effective notes while a teacher is speaking. Go over the notetaking strategies on p. 155 that apply to notetaking while listening to a speaker.

Practice/Apply

Give students a brief lesson on the same historical figure you used in the previous minilesson. Have students take notes while you speak. Have students get together in groups and compare their notes.

Journal Entry

Journal Entry

When you write a **journal entry**, you write in your notebook about anything you want, such as things you have learned or things that have happened to you.

Parts of a Journal Entry

- The date of the entry
- A beginning that introduces the topic
- A middle that includes details and your thoughts and feelings
- An ending thought

November 14

Beginning
Tells what the entry is about

People talk a lot about bullying. We've had assemblies about it at school. There are commercials about it on TV. My friends and I haven't been bullied, and we don't bully other kids. So, to be honest, I didn't think much about it. But today all of that changed.

There's a new girl in the other fifth grade class. Her name is Olga Pedraza. I don't know her very well. I guess I don't know much about any of the kids in the other fifth grade room. I mostly hang out with friends from my class.

Middle
Tells what happened and includes the writer's thoughts and feelings

Well, today in the lunchroom I saw Olga sitting alone. I probably wouldn't have noticed her except that I was hanging out by myself waiting for my best friend, Sophie. Anyhow, Olga was sitting at a table by herself drinking milk when Anthony Bain, from my class, came along with a couple of other guys. He bumped Olga's shoulder really hard, on purpose. She spilled milk all over herself. Then he called her a name and laughed.

I couldn't believe what I saw! Anthony always seems so nice when he's with my friends and me.

Dialogue makes the people and situation more real.

I wanted to walk up to him and say, "Hey, what do you think you're doing?" but I chickened out.

I did what I thought was the next best thing. I asked Olga if I could sit with her. She looked surprised and sort of scared. Then she said, "Sure." And when Sophie came, she joined us.

Olga turned out to be really nice. She and her family just moved here from Mexico City, Mexico. She told us that there are pyramids not far from where she lived. They are called the Pyramid of the Sun and the Pyramid of the Moon. I would like to see them someday. Sophie said that she would, too.

Ending
Shows how the situation wrapped up and includes a final thought

By the time lunch was over, we were friends with Olga. I can't wait to hang out with her more and meet her family.

Tomorrow, I plan to do something brave. I'm going to have a talk with Anthony Bain about bullying. Who knows, maybe when I get done with him, he'll want to be friends with Olga, too.

Note how the author of this piece:

- Used informal word choice to tell what happened.

  I mostly hang out with friends from my class.

  . . . I chickened out.

- Wrote about a meaningful experience.

  Other topics she could have written about include

  An event or concert she went to

  A favorite thing or hobby

  Something she learned about in school

  Something that happened to her

WRITING MODELS AND FORMS

Minilesson 143

Understanding the Journal Entry

Common Core State Standard: W.5.1a

Objective: Understand how to use the information about the journal entry that is presented in this lesson.

Guiding Question: How can I use these pages to help me write a journal entry?

Teach/Model

Have students read the definition and bulleted points. Explain that a journal entry allows them an opportunity to express how they feel about a topic.

Practice/Apply

Have students read pp. 156–157. Point out to students that the author uses first-person point of view and informal language in the journal entry. Ask students to describe the writer's feelings about what happened to her.

Minilesson 144

Writing About Feelings

Common Core State Standard: W.5.1a

Objective: Write about my feelings in a journal entry.

Guiding Question: How do I write about my feelings in a journal entry?

Teach/Model

Explain to students that when writing a journal entry, they should feel free to express their thoughts and feelings about the subject they focus on.

Practice/Apply

Give students a journal entry topic related to something they have learned in class recently. Ask students to write about how they can relate this topic to their own lives. Remind students to include an introduction and an ending thought in their journal entry.

Index